Foundational Snare Drumming

By James Weaver

Foundational Snare Drumming

Focusing on the Essentials

By James Weaver

This book was written to focus on the skills that are the most important in establishing a solid foundation. The sequence of the book is critical and each concept/skill should be mastered before moving on.

Use the Play Along Tracks for the exercises that have them but only once they are mastered. It is appropriate to use a metronome at all times when not playing with the Play Along Tracks.

For ease of use with the Play Along Tracks, feel free to email me and request a digital copy of that page with clickable links.

jaweaver@mbgsd.org

Foundational Snare Drumming
Play Along Tracks

Rebound Stroke Practice:

Slow: https://safeyoutube.net/w/MXZo
Medium: https://safeyoutube.net/w/2YZo
Fast: https://safeyoutube.net/w/TYZo

Quarter Note Exercises:

Lesson 2.1:   https://safeyoutube.net/w/UZZo
Lesson 2.2:   https://safeyoutube.net/w/Kaap
Lesson 2.3   https://safeyoutube.net/w/Rbap
Lesson 2.4:   https://safeyoutube.net/w/Bcap
Lesson 2.5:   https://safeyoutube.net/w/hdap

Eighth Note Exercises:

Lesson 3.1:   https://safeyoutube.net/w/XAep
Lesson 3.2:   https://safeyoutube.net/w/zEkp
Lesson 3.3:   https://safeyoutube.net/w/YFqp
Lesson 3.4:   https://safeyoutube.net/w/ZGqp
Lesson 3.5:   https://safeyoutube.net/w/6Hqp

Sixteenth Note Exercises:

Lesson 4.1:   https://safeyoutube.net/w/yj3t`
Lesson 4.2:   https://safeyoutube.net/w/or6p
Lesson 4.3:   https://safeyoutube.net/w/Zq6p
Lesson 4.4:   https://safeyoutube.net/w/Kq6p
Lesson 4.5:   https://safeyoutube.net/w/8q6p

1 Eighth and 2 Sixteenth Note Exercises:

Lesson 5.1:   https://safeyoutube.net/w/sq6p
Lesson 5.2:   https://safeyoutube.net/w/hq6p
Lesson 5.3:   https://safeyoutube.net/w/Pp6p
Lesson 5.4:   https://safeYouTube.net/w/8p6p
Lesson 5.5:   https://safeyoutube.net/w/vp6p

2 Sixteenth and 1 Eighth Note Exercises

Lesson 6.1:   https://safeyoutube.net/w/jp6p
Lesson 6.2:   https://safeyoutube.net/w/Mo6p
Lesson 6.3:   https://safeyoutube.net/w/xo6p
Lesson 6.4:   https://safeyoutube.net/w/dvVt
Lesson 6.5:   https://safeYouTube.net/w/Jn6p

*To obtain a digital copy of this page for quick access to the links, email your request to jaweaver@mbgsd.org.

Unit 1

Beginning Snare Drum Grip

The Grip: (Matched Grip = Hands Mirror each other)

To set the grip, start by establishing the fulcrum (pivot point). This is typically around 2/3's of the way down the stick but can vary from stick to stick.

- Pinch between your thumb and first knuckle.

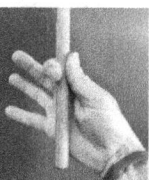

- This is the most important contact point in your grip.

- The pinch should be firm but not to the point of causing tension. As you progress, the tension of this pinch will vary depending on the stroke you are using.

- Have the back end of your stick follow through the center of your palm (This is just a guide and is not exact on everyone's hands. Your instructor will advise you if you need to adjust this at all.)

- Wrap your remaining fingers around the stick with as little tension as possible. Visualize the fingers becoming less important as they move down to the pinky. Make sure they are all making contact with the stick.

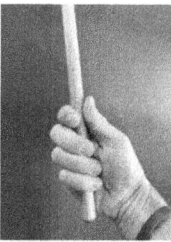

- Please see this video for extra instruction:
- http://safeyoutube.net/w/pOYe

The First Snare Drum Stroke

Rebound Stroke:

The foundation for snare drumming starts with this stroke.

- Think of a ball bouncing off of the ground. The ball will come back up on its own unless something keeps if from coming up.

- Wrists and fingers should be completely relaxed.

- You should not need to "lift" the stick to get back to the starting point of the stroke. The stick should bounce back easily. If this is not occurring, you are applying too much tension.

- Follow this link for a video demonstration of the rebound stroke.

http://safeyoutube.net/w/Ny6g

*Make sure to practice unit 1 for a full week before you start trying to read music!

Once you feel comfortable with the stroke, try the sticking patterns on the next couple pages.

Lesson 1.1

(Play each line TWO times)

Line #1

R R R R   R R R R   R R R R   R R R R

Line #2

L L L L   L L L L   L L L L   L L L L

Line #3

R R R R   L L L L   R R R R   L L L L

Line #4

R R L L   R R L L   R R L L   R R L L

Line #5

R L R L   R L R L   R L R L   R L R L

Lesson 1.2

(Play each line TWO times)

Line #6

R R R L   R R R L   R R R L   R R R L

Line #7

L L L R   L L L R   L L L R   L L L R

Line #8

R L R R   L R L L   R L R R   L R L L

Line #9

L R L L   R L R R   L R L L   R L R R

Line #10

R L L R   L R R L   R L L R   L R R L

Lesson 1.3

(Play each line TWO times)

Line #11

RRLR   LLRL   RRLR   LLRL

Line #12

RLLL   RLLL   LRRR   LRRR

*Once you mastered these patterns, visit the Play Along Tracks links page. You will find three different speeds to practice. Start with the slowest speed and work your way up to the fastest speed. Do not rush the process. Make sure each speed is mastered before trying the next!

Musical Symbols

Percussion Clef: ─‖─

The Percussion Clef consists of two parallel lines. This clef is used to indicate that non-pitched percussion instruments are to be played.

Staff:

In the beginning units we will be using a single line staff. As you progress, you will be introduced to a 5 line staff.

Measure/Bar lines:

A measure is the space on a staff between two bar lines. Each measure is given a specific amount of counts.

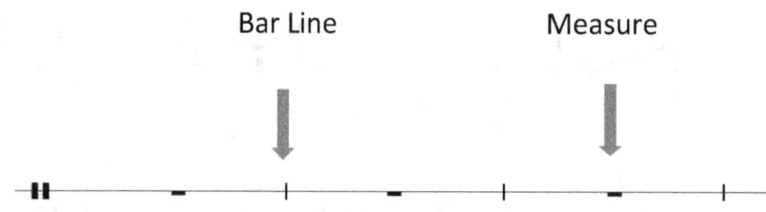

Repeat Sign: ─:‖

This symbol means to repeat the exercise. As you advance you will be introduced to beginning and ending repeats.

Time Signature:

The time signature is at the beginning of each exercise and shows the number of counts per measure and what note gets one count.

4 - The top number tells us how many counts per measure (In this case 4)
4 - A "4" on the bottom tells us that the Quarter Note equals one count.

Unit 2

The 1/4 Note and Rest

A single quarter note looks like this:

A single quarter rest looks like this:

The quarter note will receive one beat of sound.

The quarter rest will receive one beat of silence.

The general rule is that if the quarter note occurs on an odd count it is played with the right hand and if it occurs on an even count it is played with the left hand.

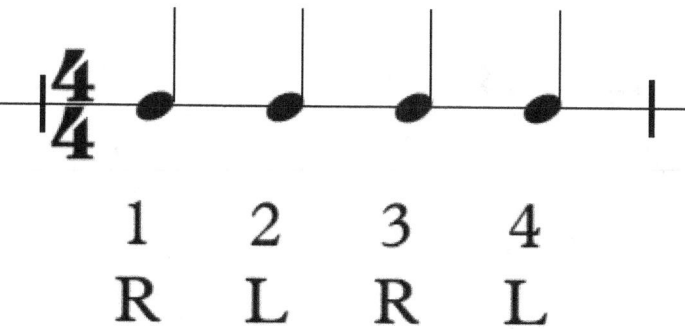

Lesson 2.1

1

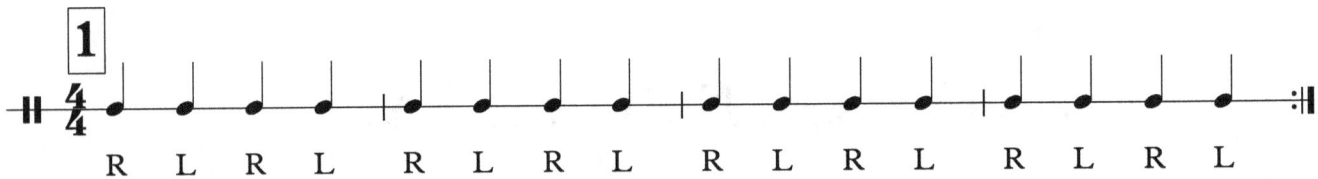

R L R L R L R L R L R L R L R L

2

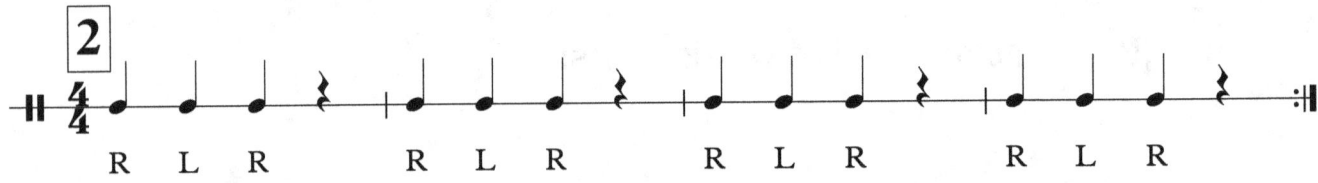

R L R R L R R L R R L R

3

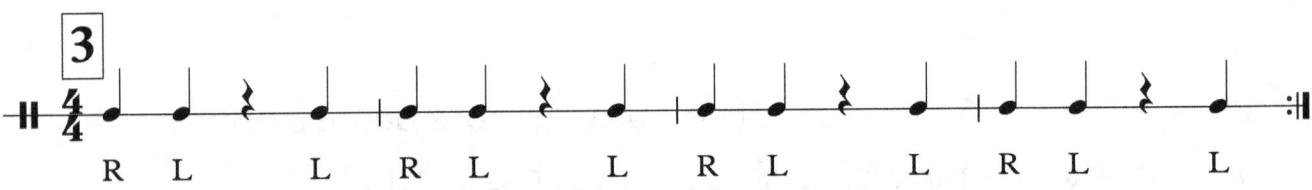

R L L L R L L R L L L R L L

4

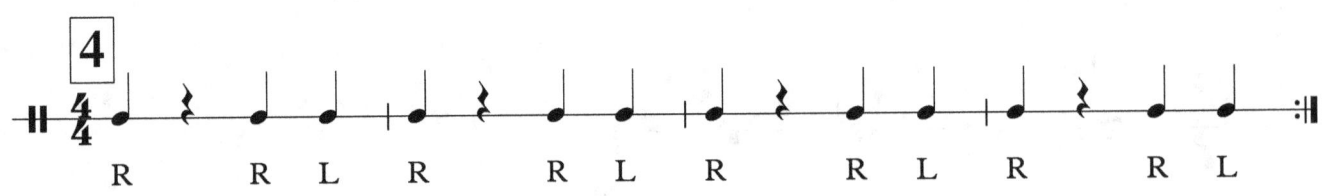

R R L R R L R R L R R L

5

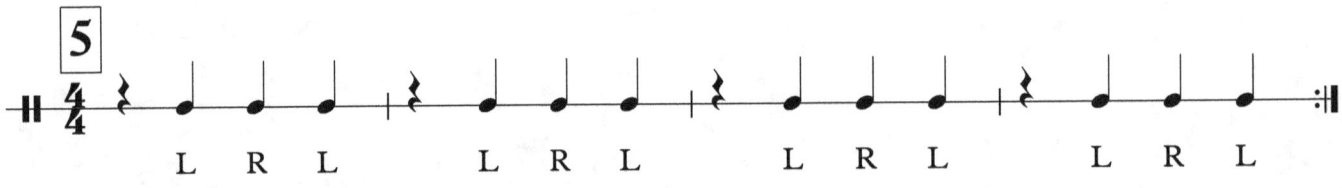

L R L L R L L R L L R L

Lesson 2.2

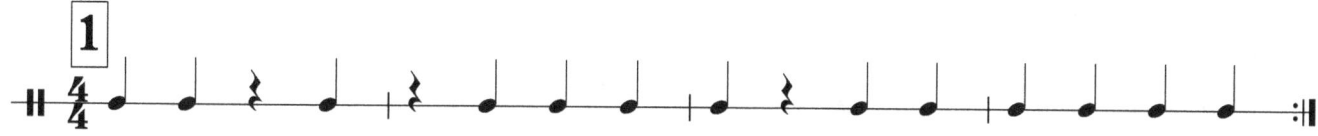

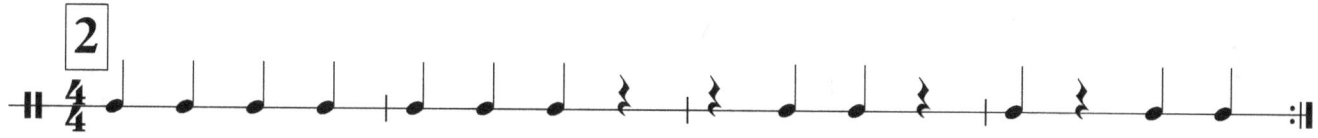

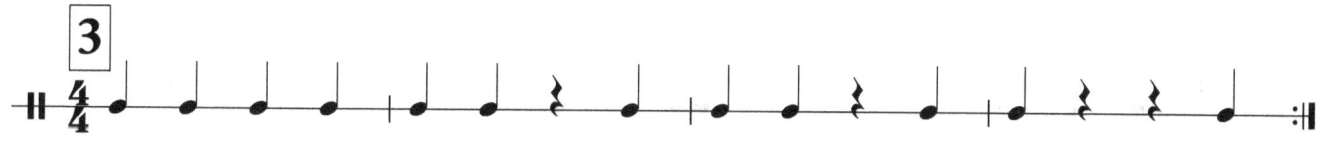

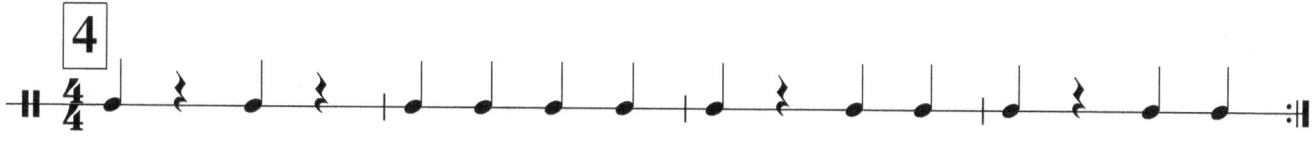

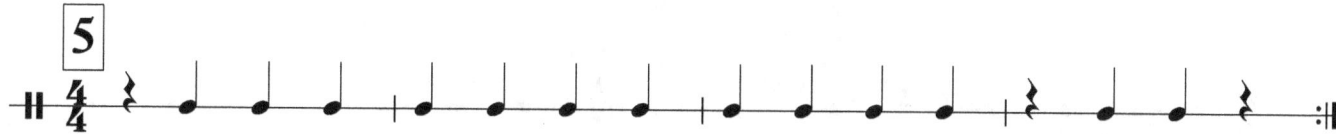

Lesson 2.3

1
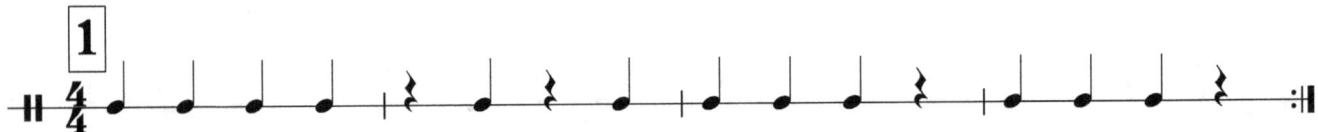

2
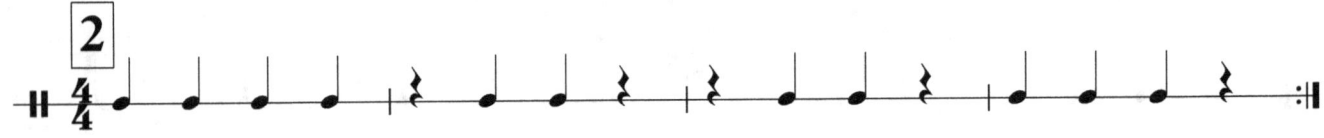

3
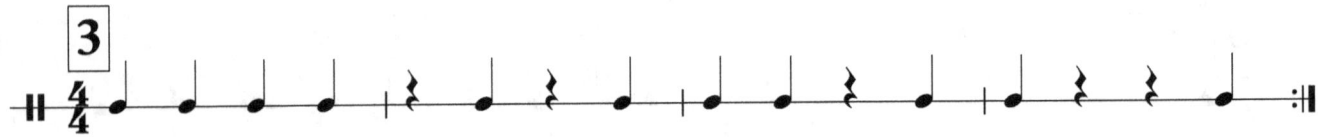

4
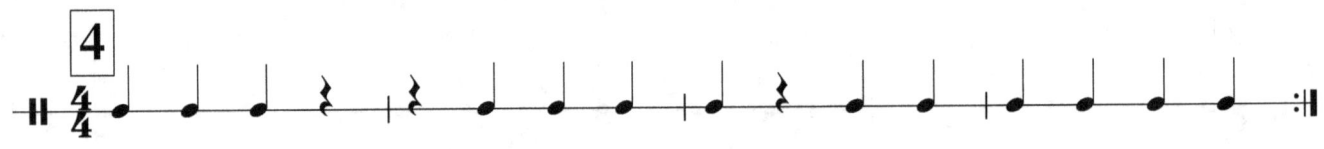

5
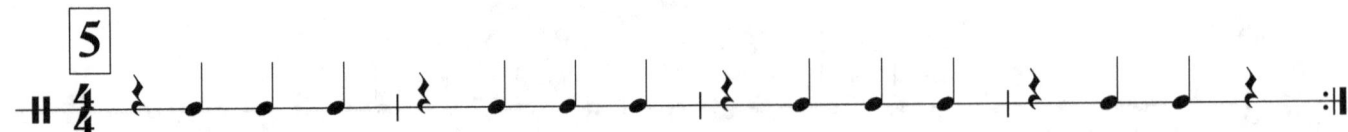

Lesson 2.4

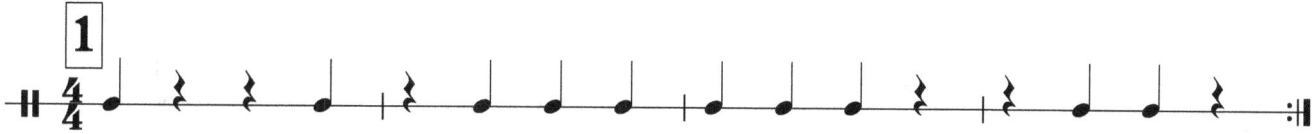

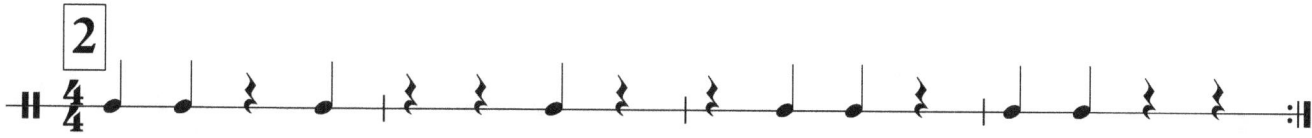

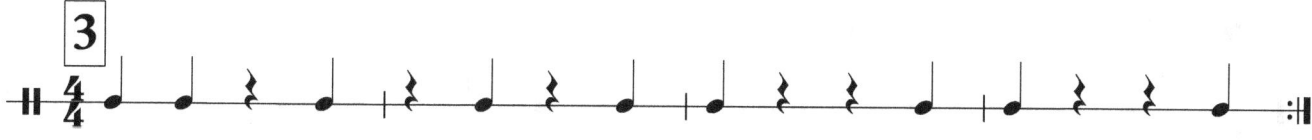

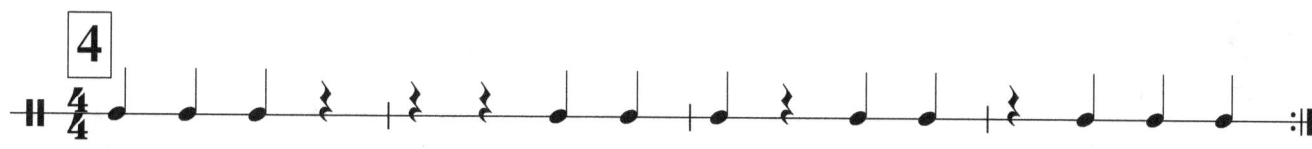

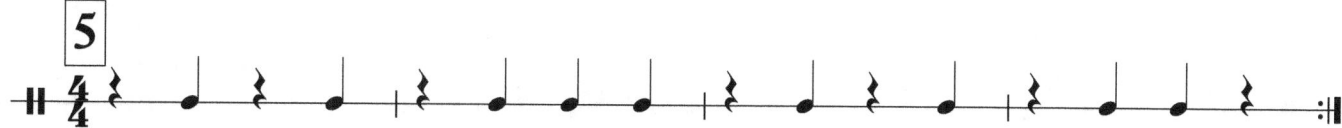

Lesson 2.5

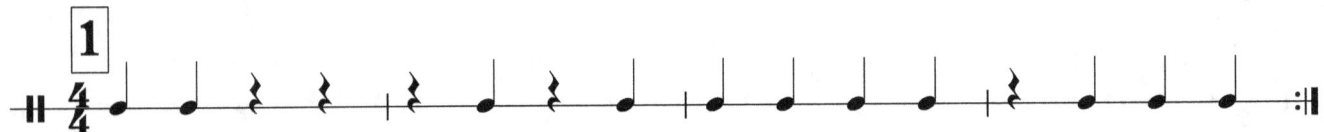

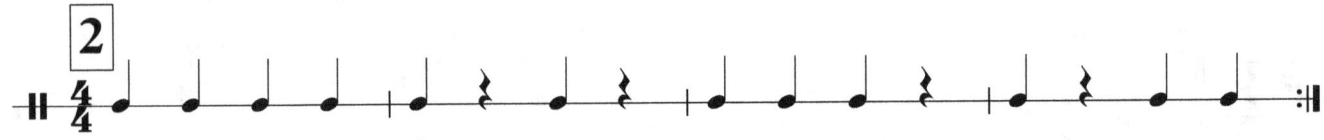

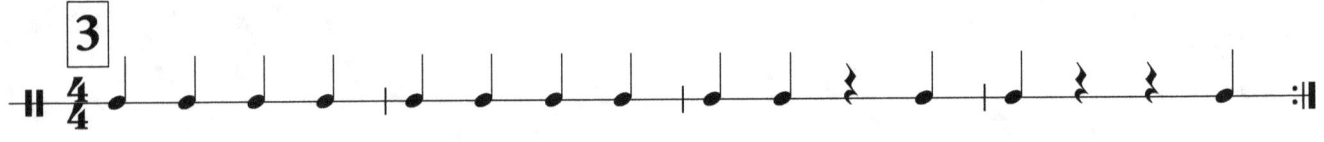

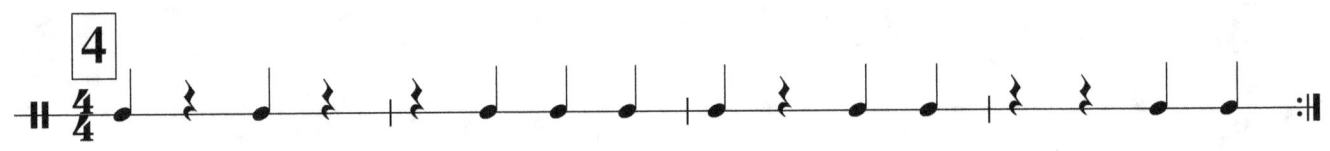

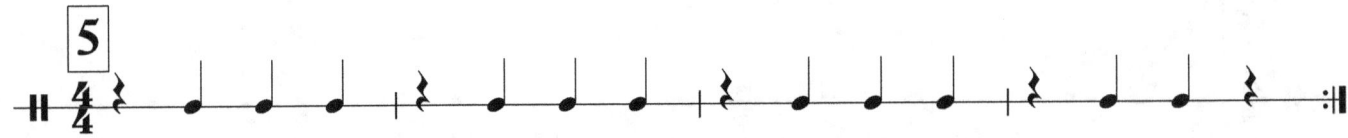

Lesson 2.6

***There is not a background track for this page. You should use a metronome to keep a steady beat. Start at 100 BPM and work up to 140 BPM.

1

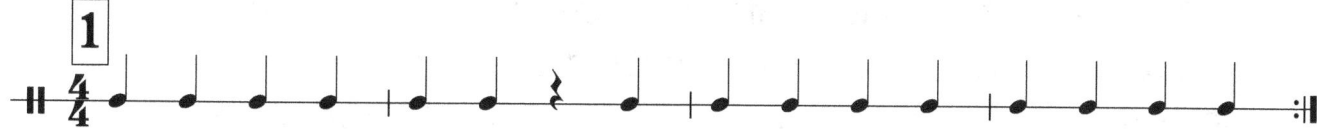

2

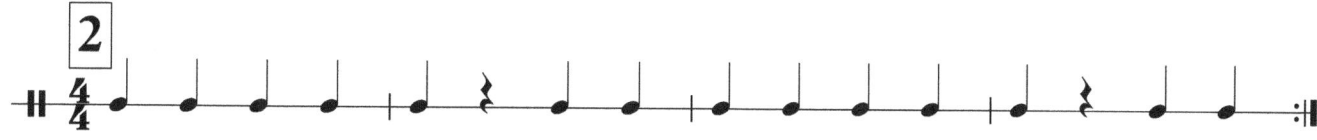

3

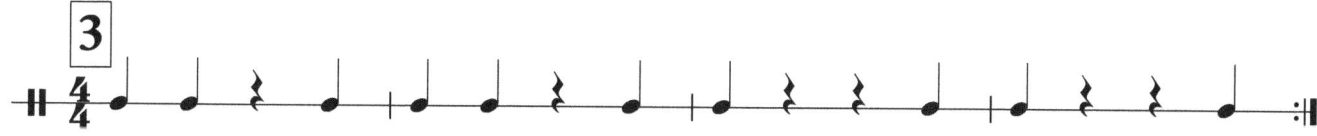

4

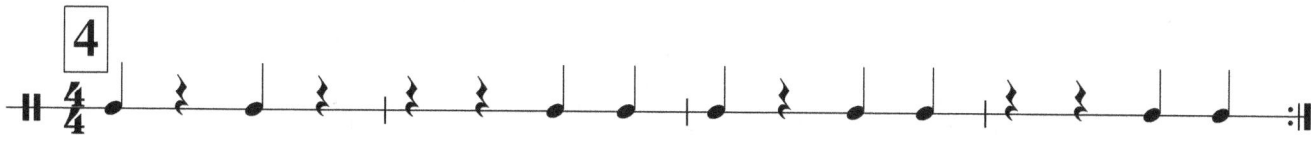

5

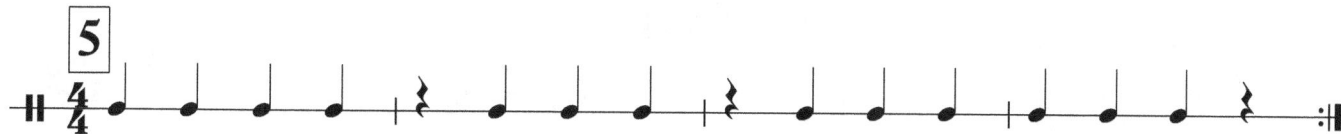

Changing Time Signatures

In the next page of exercises, there are two new time signatures. Notice that they both still have a 4 on the bottom. This means that we will still count and stick rhythms the same way. The only thing that will change is the number of counts in each measure.

4   - 4 counts per Measure
4   - Quarter note = 1 count

3   - 3 Counts per Measure
4   - Quarter note = 1 count

2   - 2 Counts per Measure
4   - Quarter note = 1 count

Lesson 2.7

There is not a Play Along Track for this page! Use a metronome to keep a steady beat. Start at 100 BPM and work up to 140 BPM.

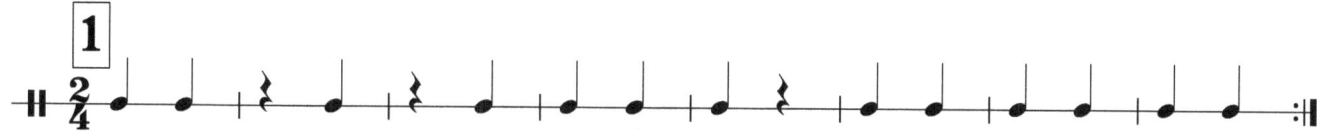

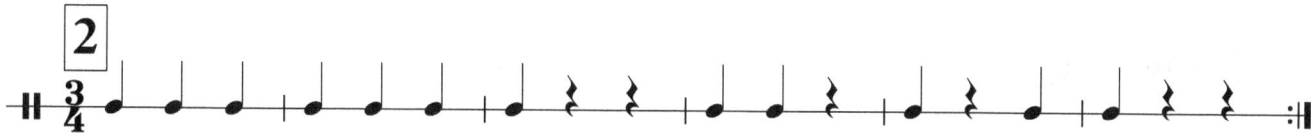

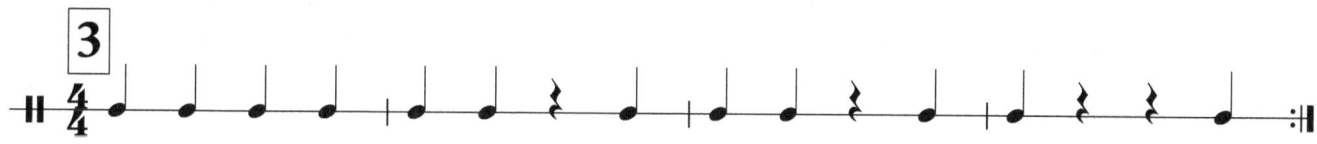

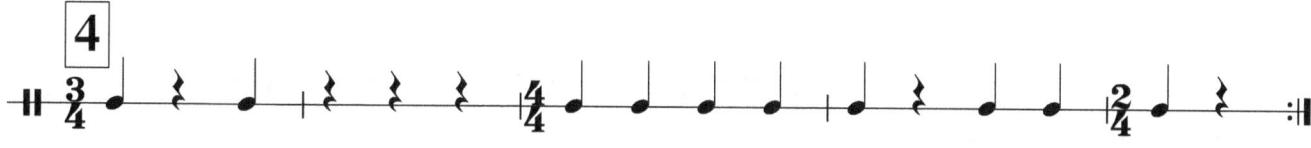

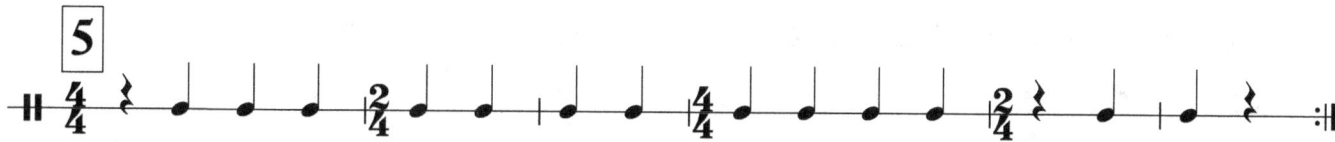

Unit 3

The Eighthth Note

A single eighth note looks like this: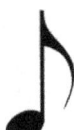

A single eighth note takes up 1/2 of a beat.

We are going to start by learning and practicing groups of at least 2 eighth notes combined.   We will combine them with a single beam.

2 eighth notes combined look like this: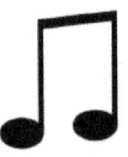

No matter what beat this rhythm occurs on, we will stick it the same way: R-L

This rhythm is counted by giving the first note the beat that it occurs on followed by &.
For example, if this rhythm is on beat two, it would be counted 2-&.

Lesson 3.1

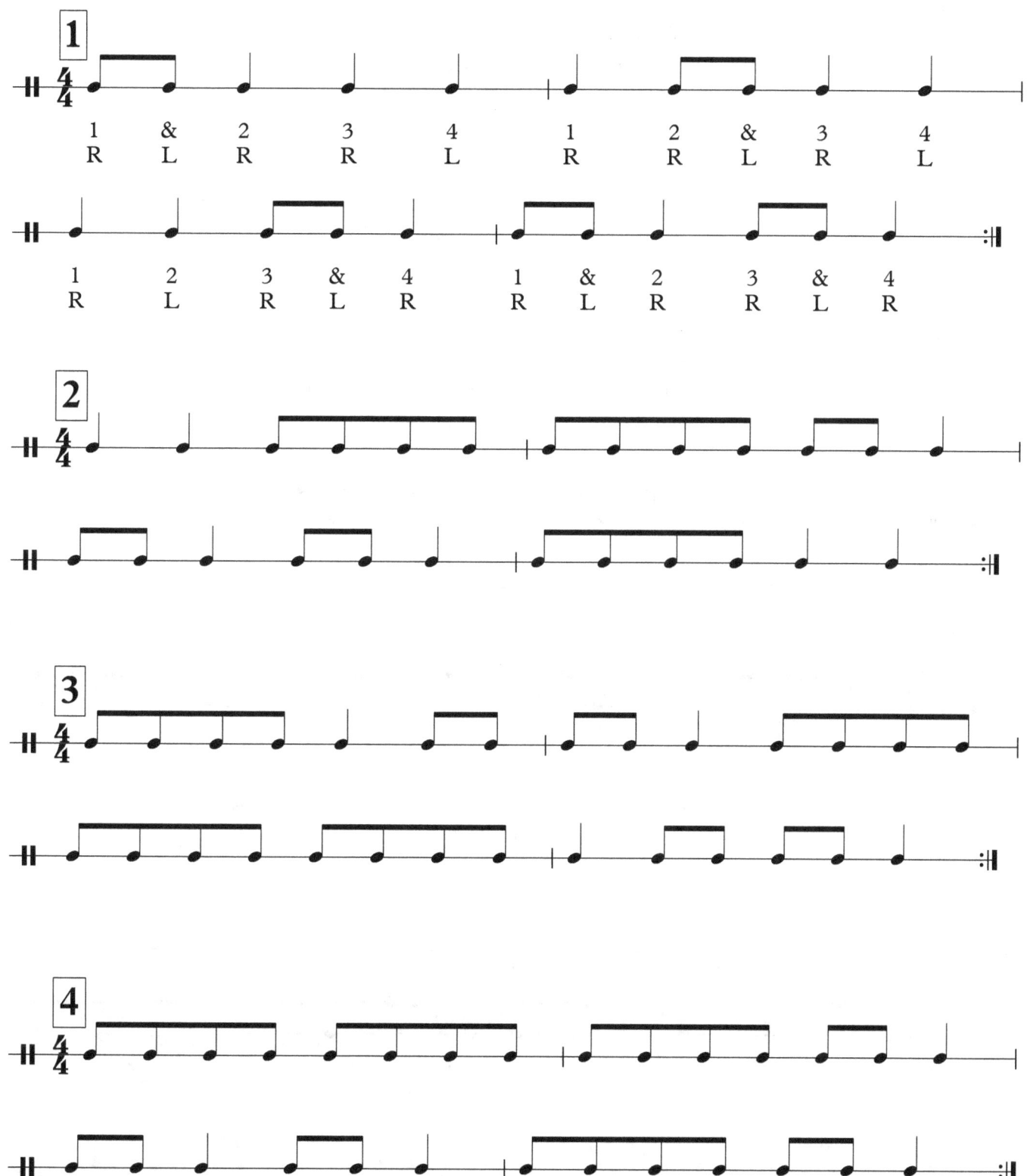

Lesson 3.2

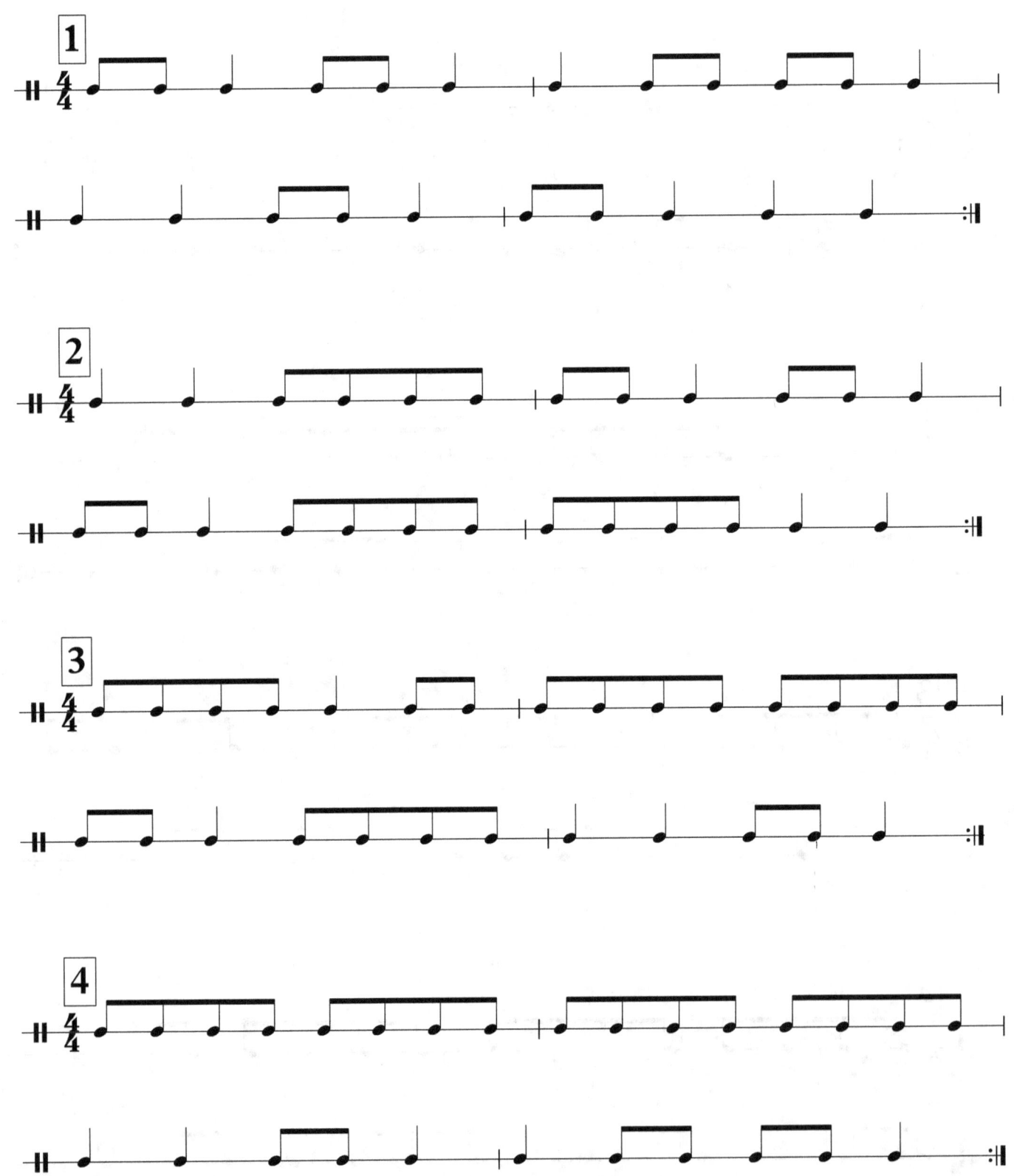

Lesson 3.3

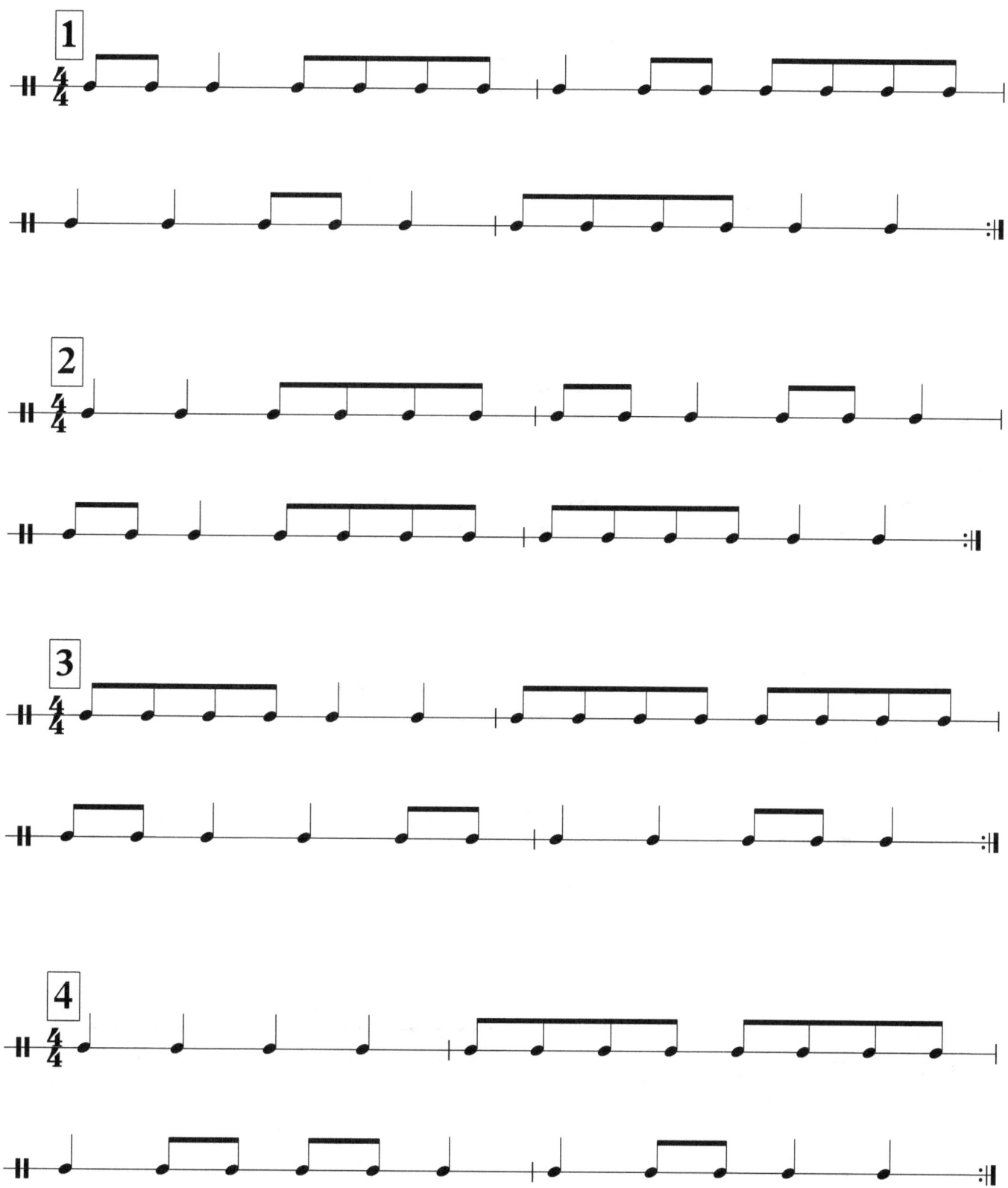

Lesson 3.4

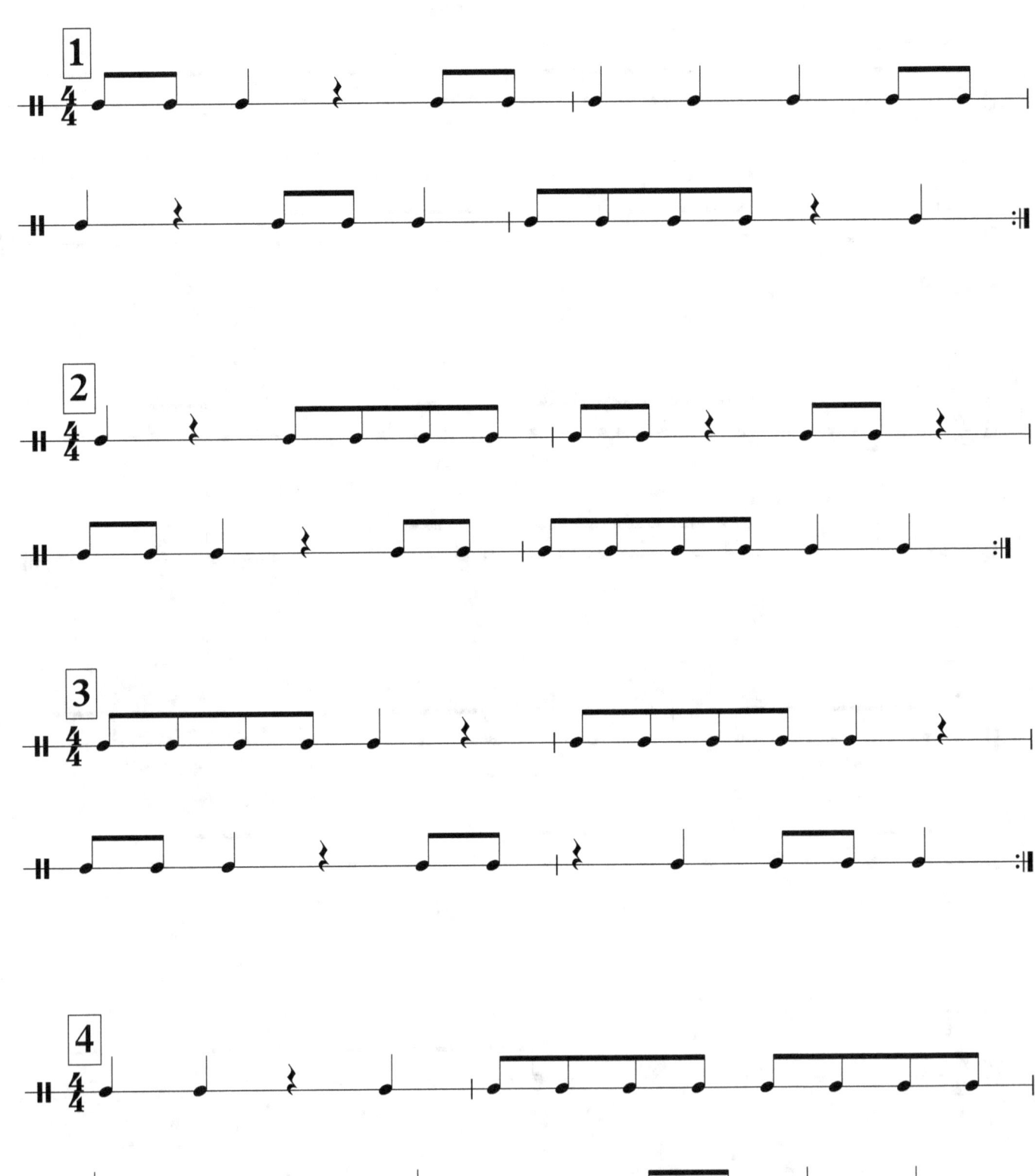

Lesson 3.5

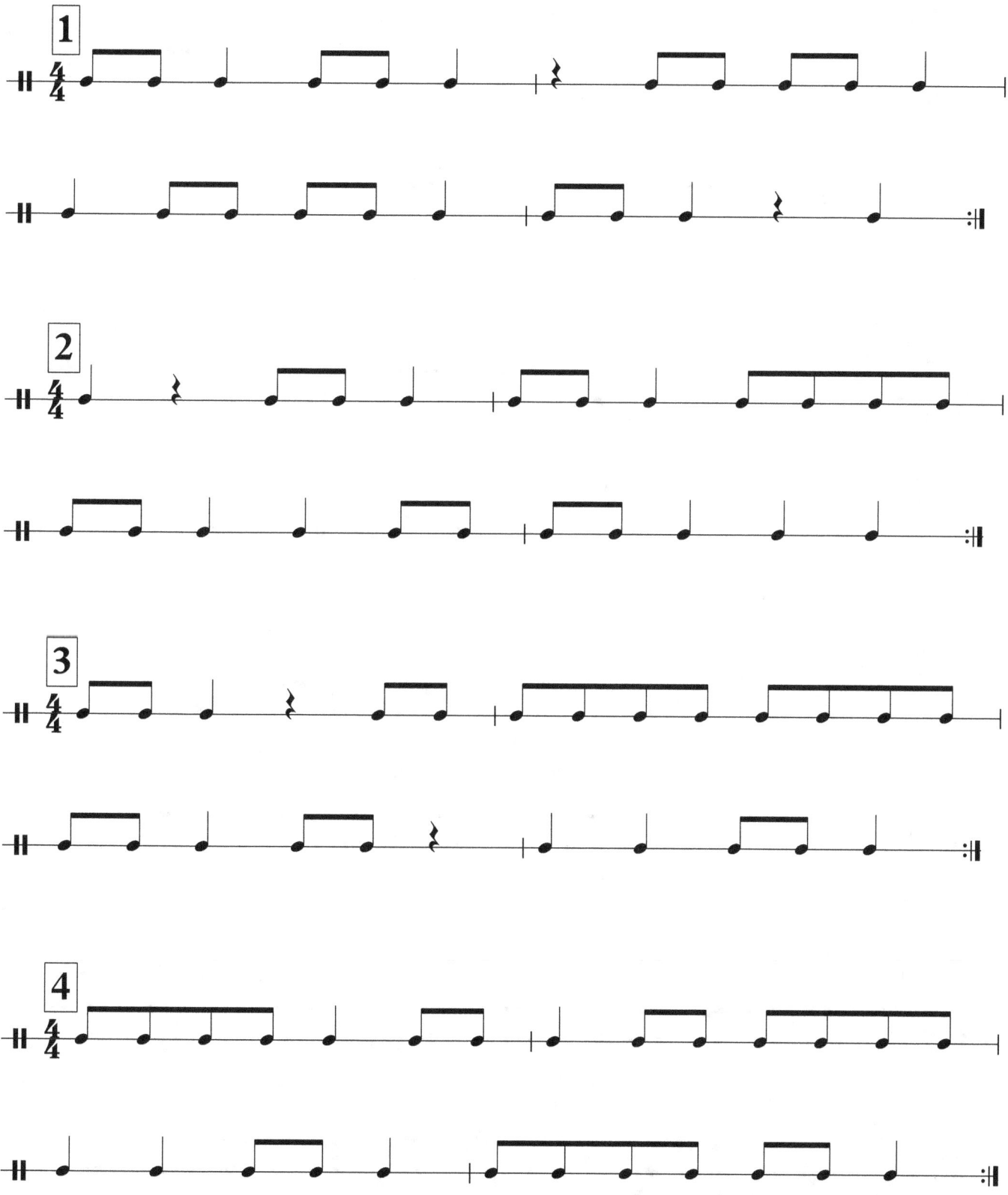

Lesson 3.6

*There is not a Play Along Track for this page. Use a metronome to keep a steady beat. Start at 80 BPM and work up to 120 BPM.

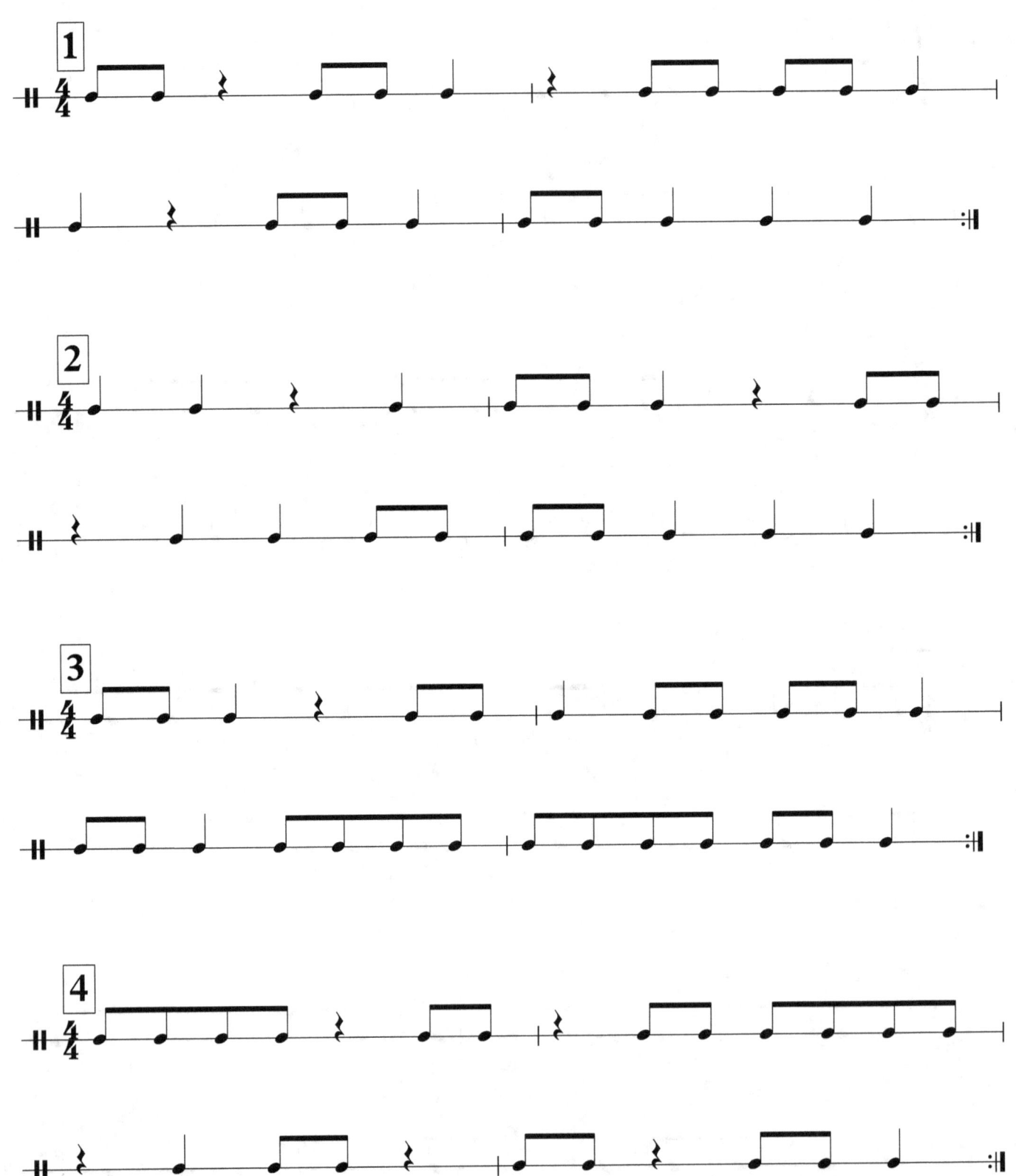

Lesson 3.7

***There is not a play along track for this page! You should use a metronome to keep a steady beat. Start at 80 BPM and work up to 120 BPM.

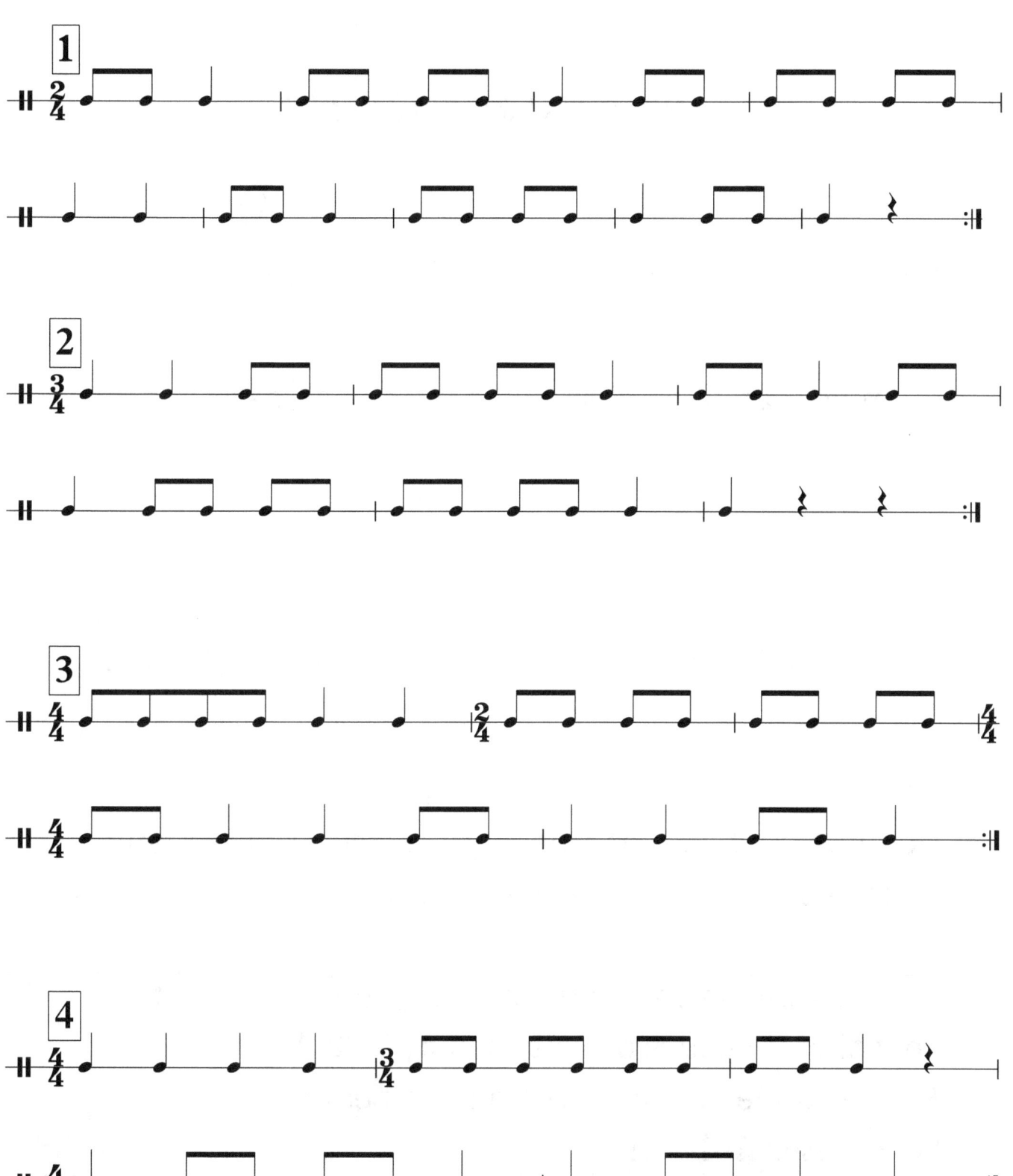

Unit 4

The Sixteenth Note

A single sixteenth note looks like this: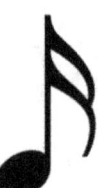

A single sixteenth note takes up ¼ of a beat.

4 sixteenth notes combined look like this: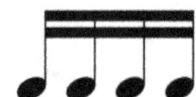

No matter what beat this rhythm occurs on, it will be sticked the same way: R-L-R-L

This rhythm is counted by giving the first note the beat that it occurs on followed by E-&-A.
For example, if this rhythm is on beat two, it would be counted 2-E-&-A.

Lesson 4.1

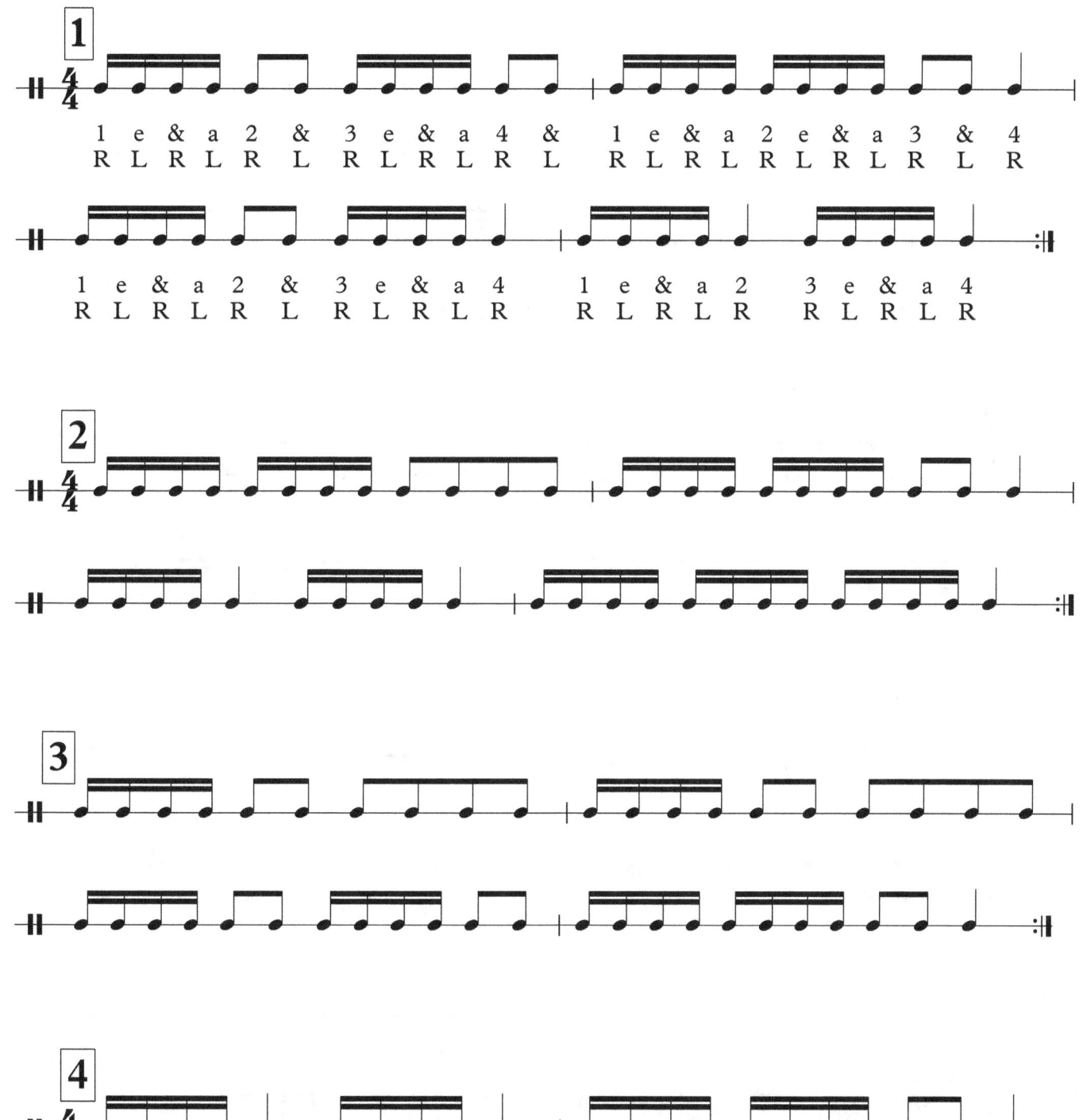

Lesson 4.2

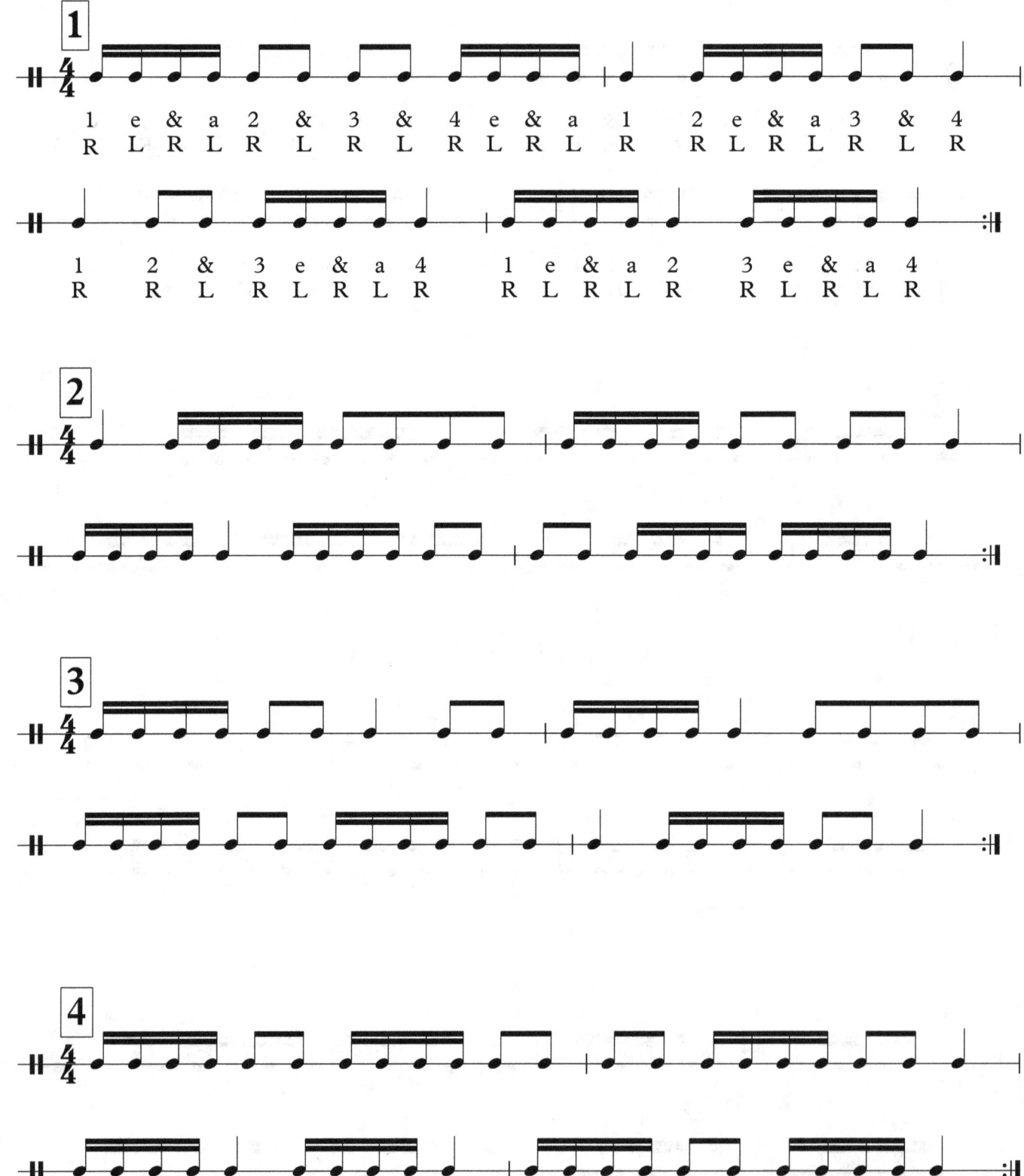

Lesson 4.3

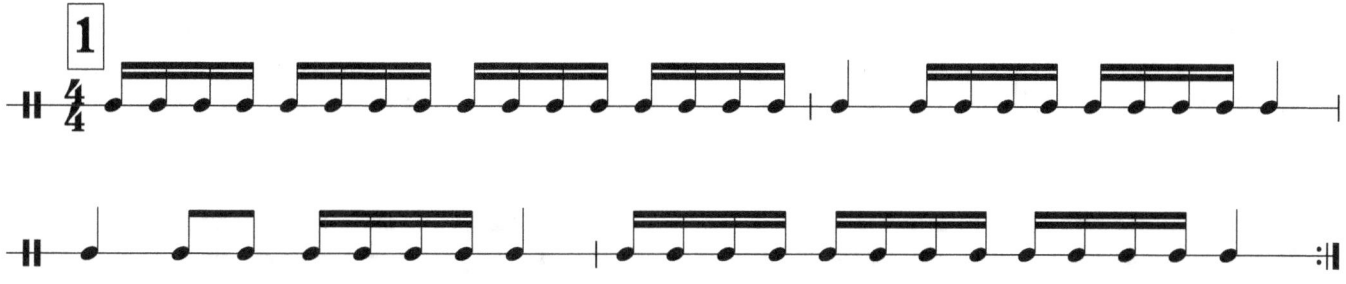

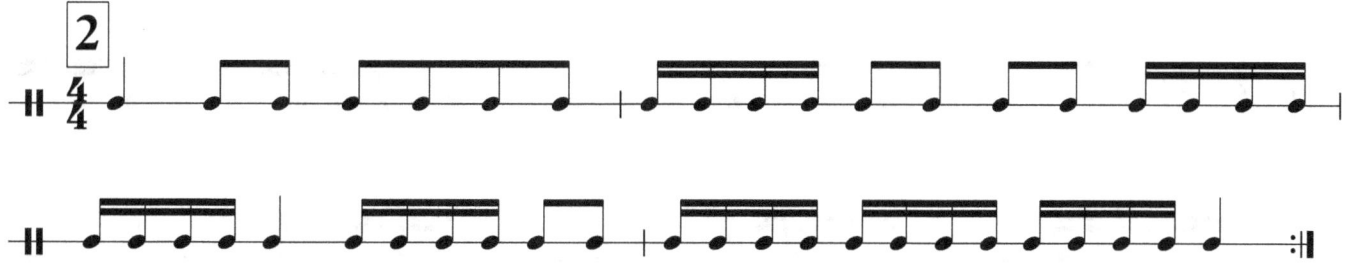

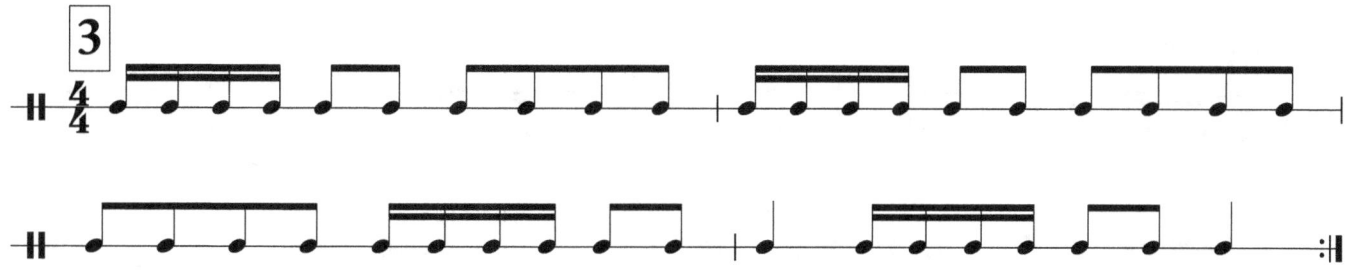

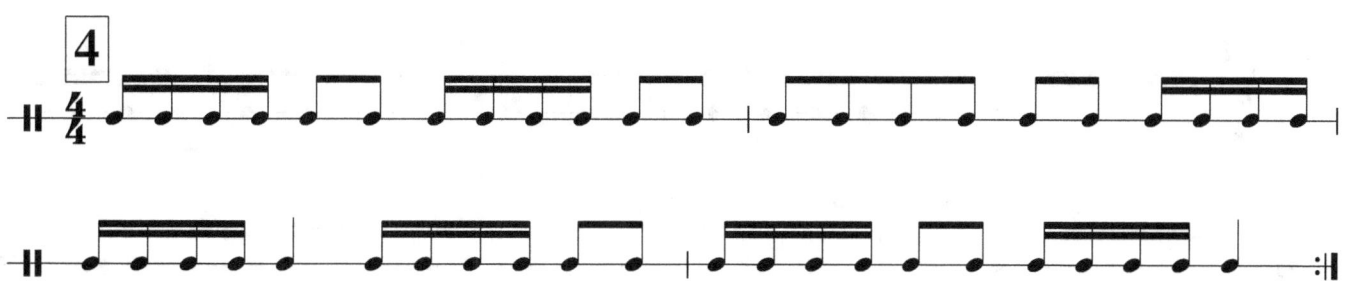

Lesson 4.4

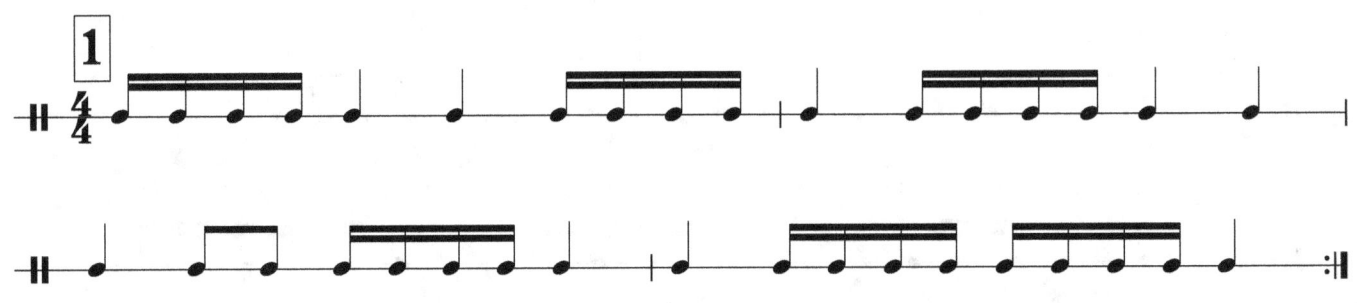

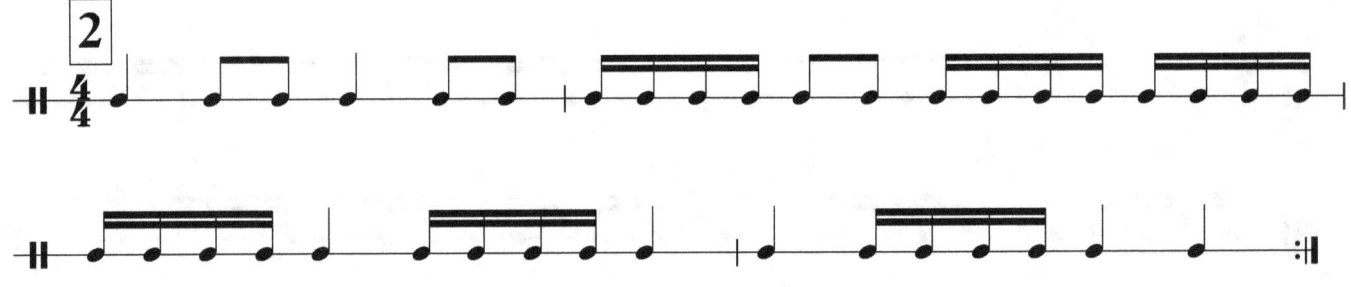

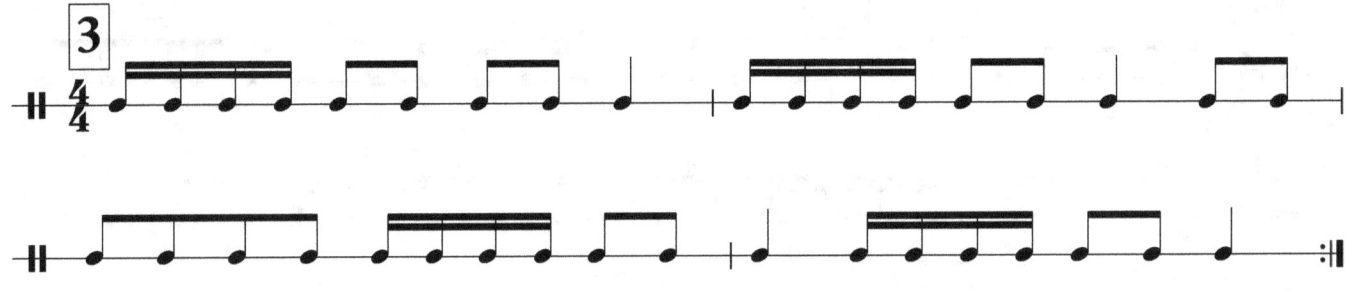

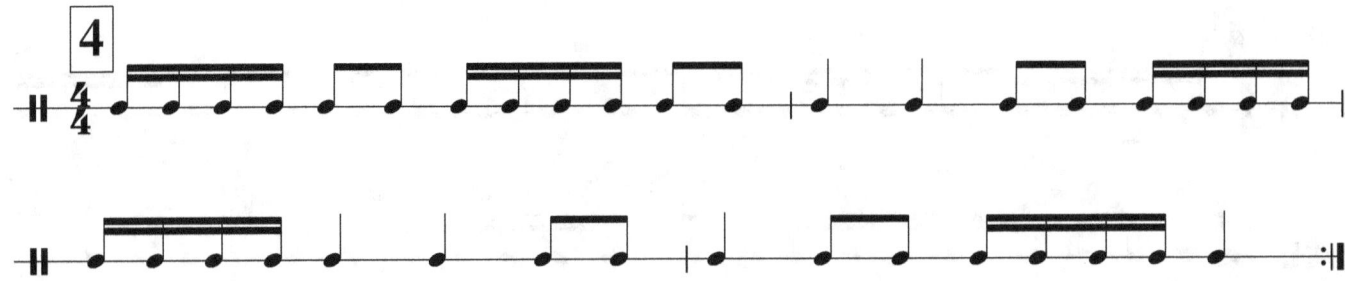

Lesson 4.5

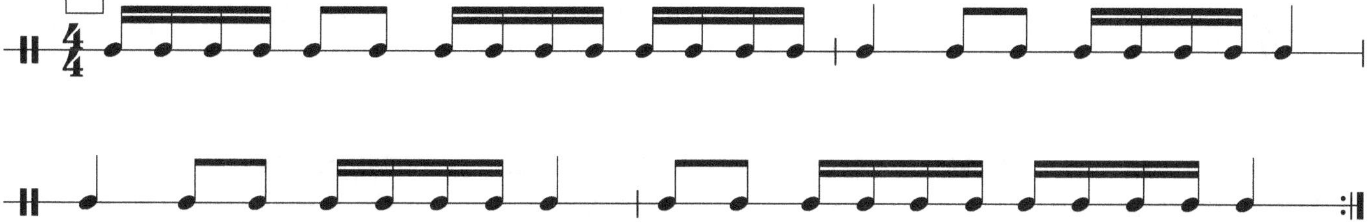

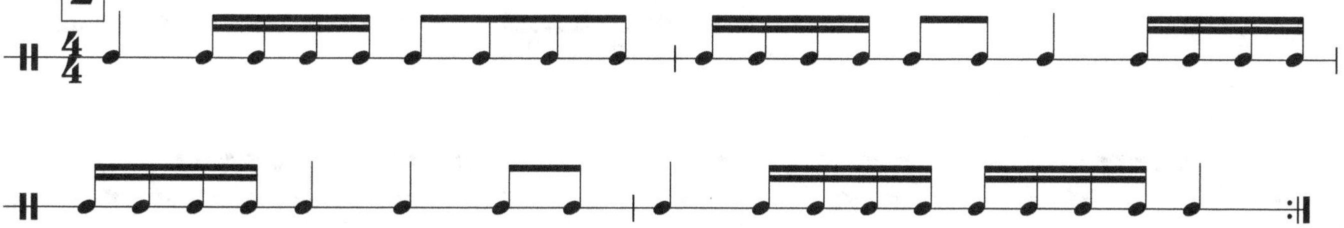

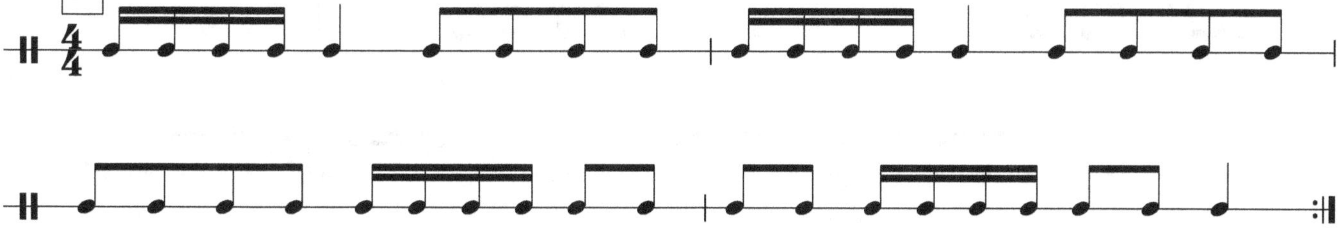

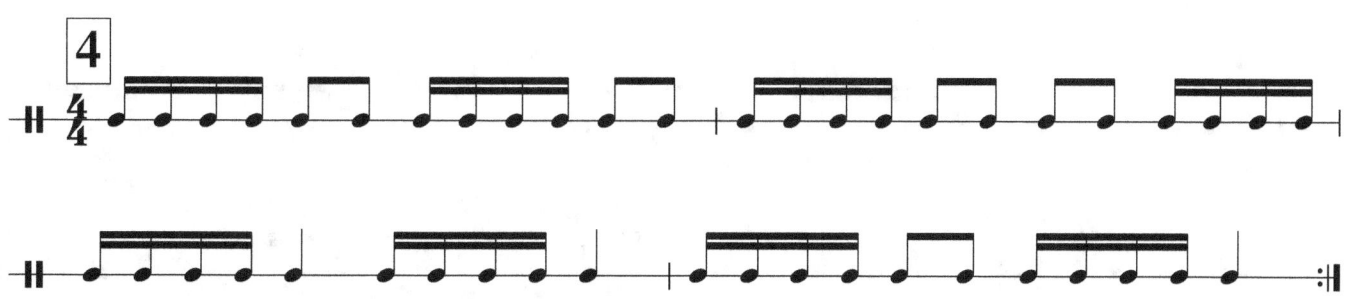

Lesson 4.6

*There is not a Play Along Track for this page! Use a metronome to keep a steady beat. Start at 80 BPM and work up to 110 BPM.

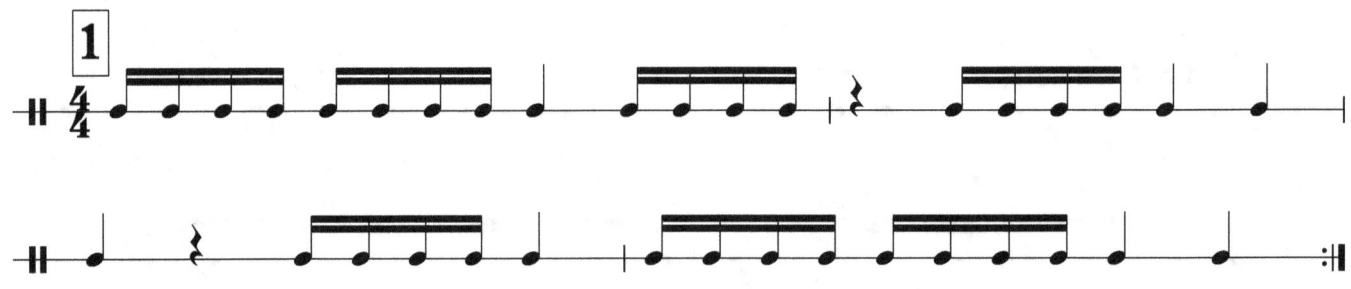

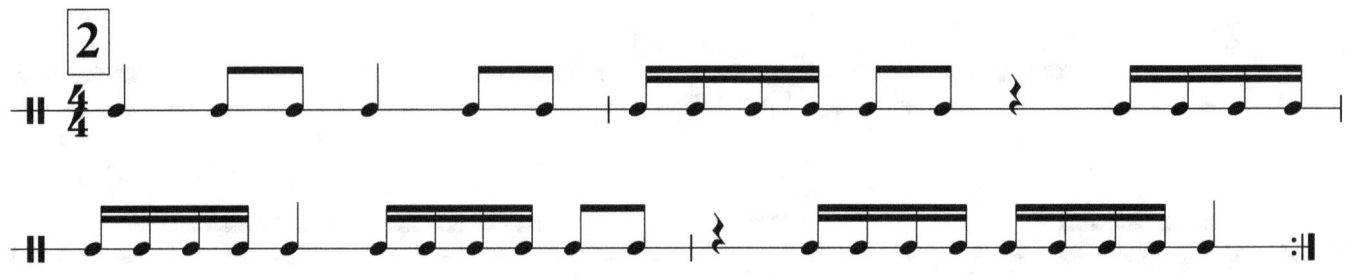

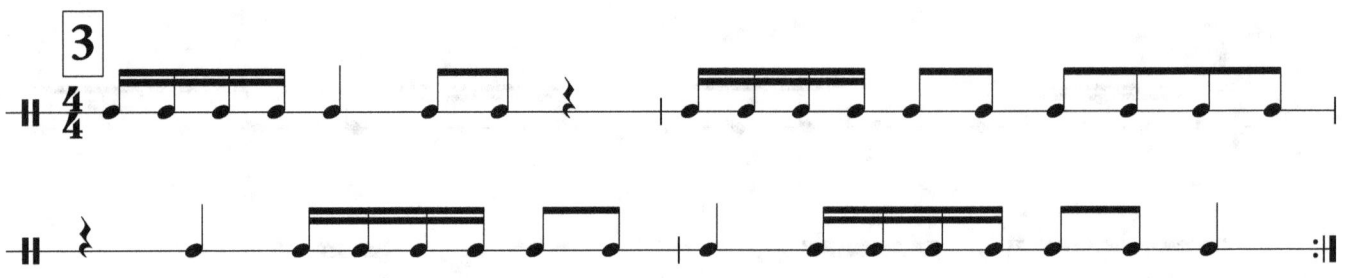

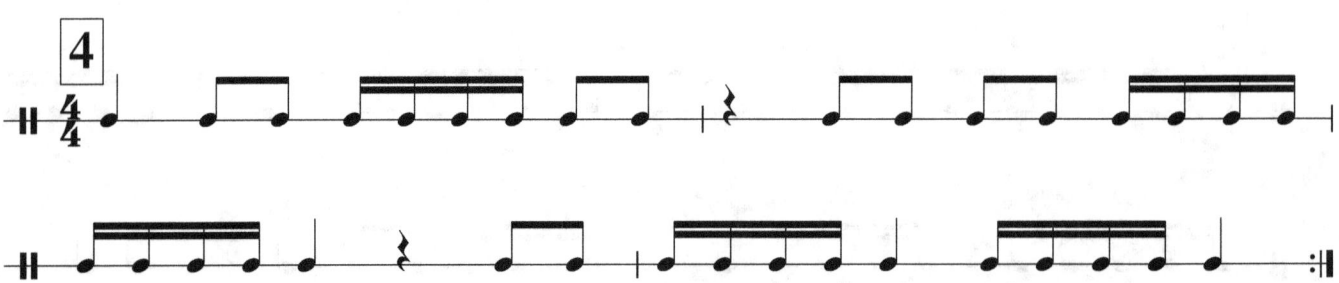

Lesson 4.7

*There is not a Play Along Track for this page! Use a metronome to keep a steady beat. Start at 80 BPM and work up to 110 BPM.

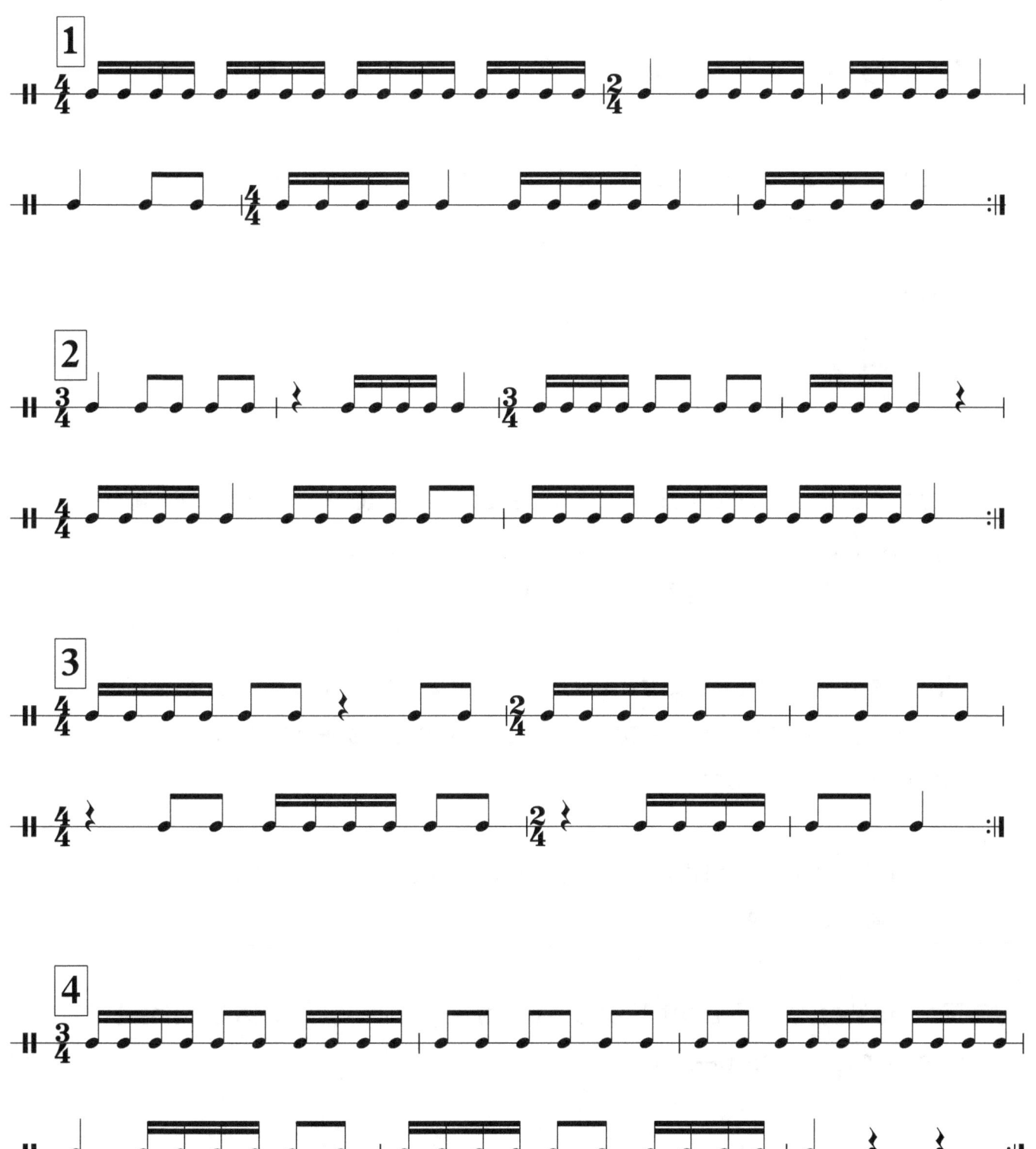

Unit 5

Sixteenth Notes and Eighth Notes Combined

This is what one eighth and two sixteenth notes look
like when combined:

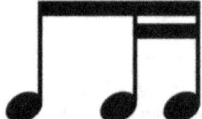

This combination takes up one beat. The eighth note takes
up the first half of the beat and the two sixteenth notes
take up the second half of the beat.

This is counted by giving the eighth note the number of
whatever beat it falls on and the two sixteenths will
always get the counts &-A.

For example, if this rhythm is on beat two, it would be
counted 2--&-A.

No matter what beat this rhythm occurs on, it is sticked
the same way: R--R-L

Lesson 5.1

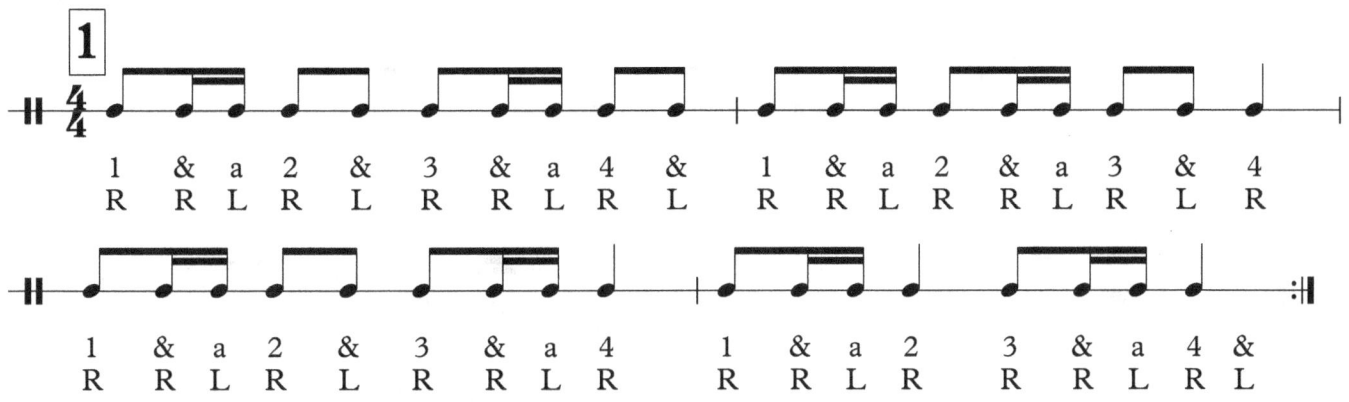

1 & a 2 & 3 & a 4 &
R R L R L R R L R L

1 & a 2 & 3 & a 4
R R L R L R R L R

1 & a 2 & a 3 & 4
R R L R R L R L R

1 & a 2 3 & a 4 &
R R L R R R L R L

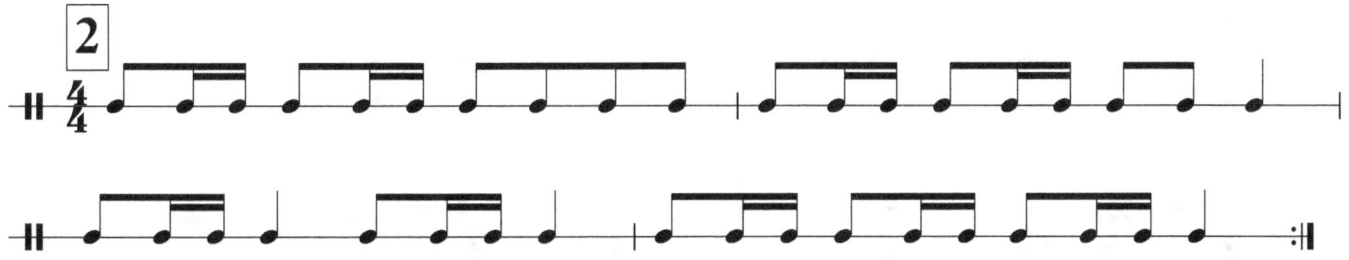

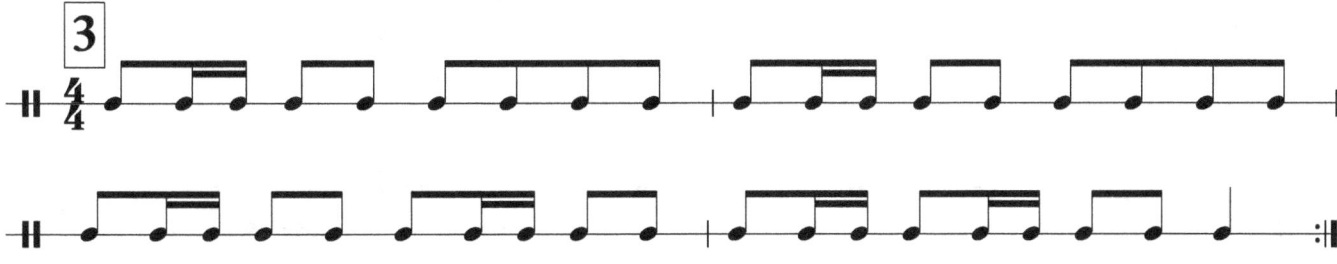

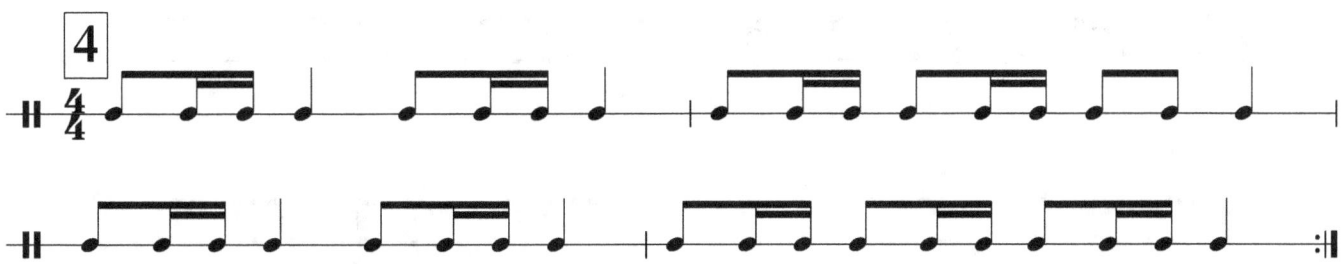

Lesson 5.2

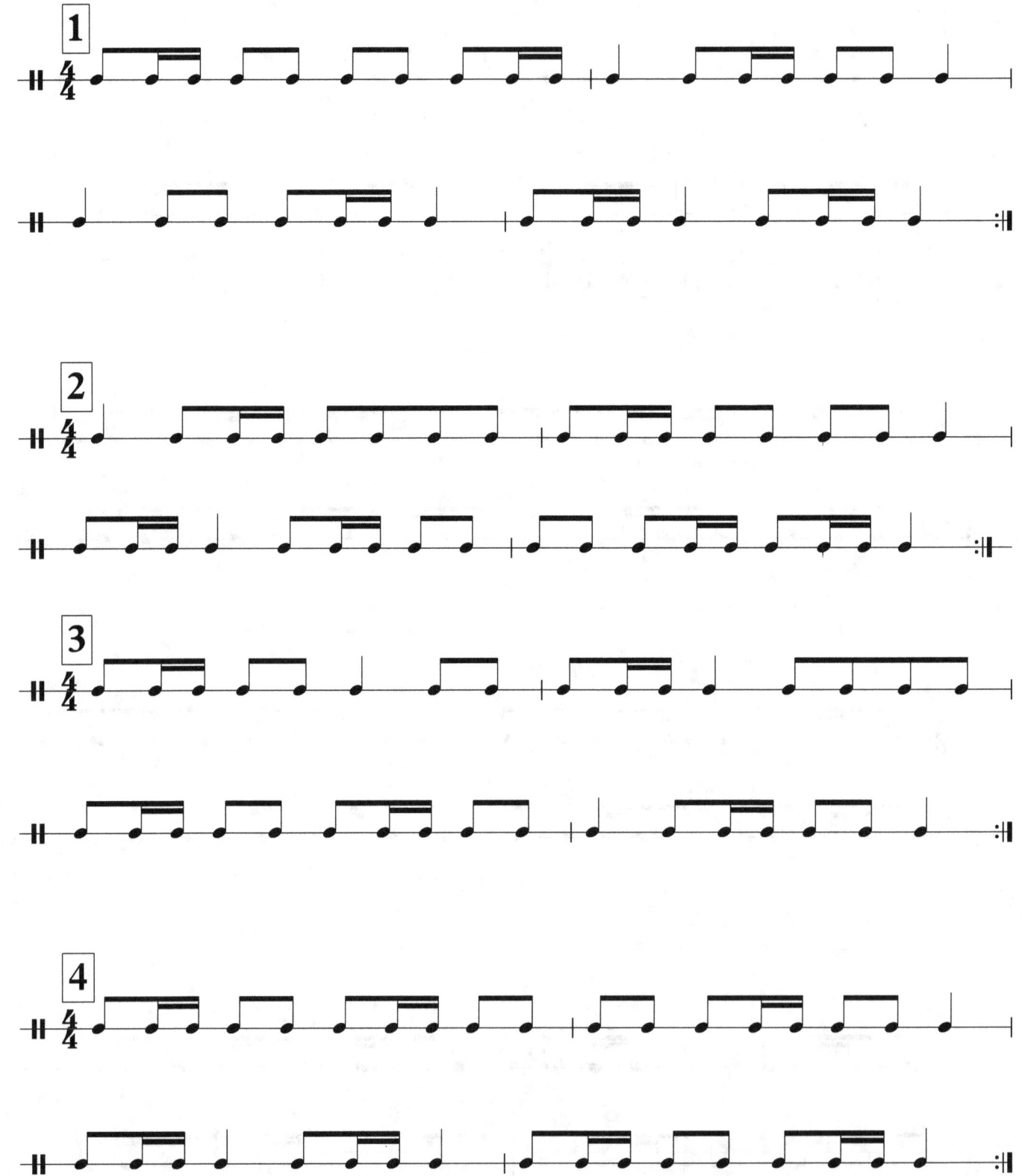

Lesson 5.3

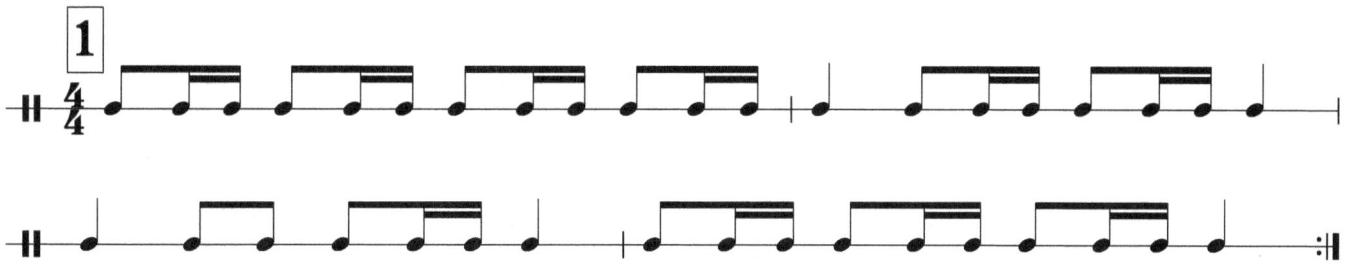

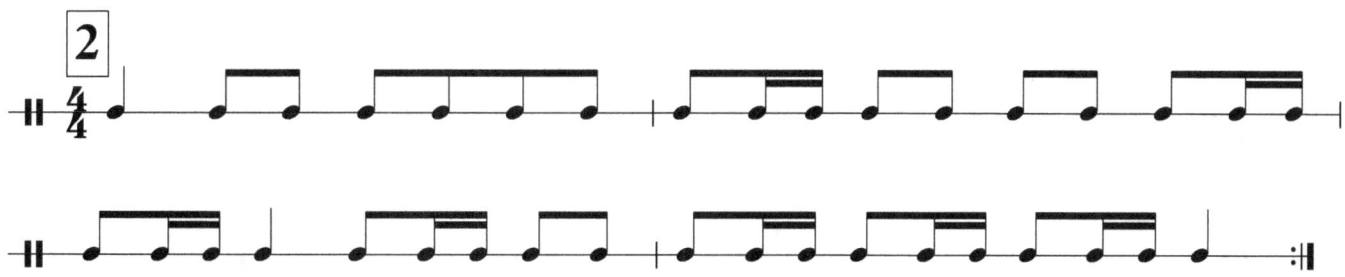

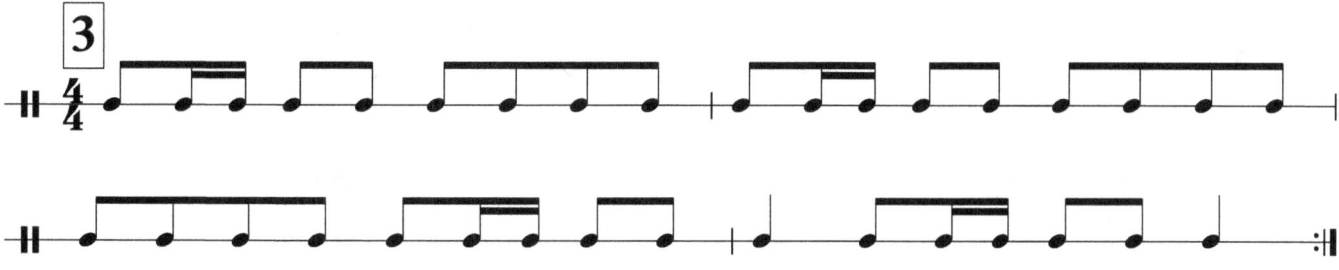

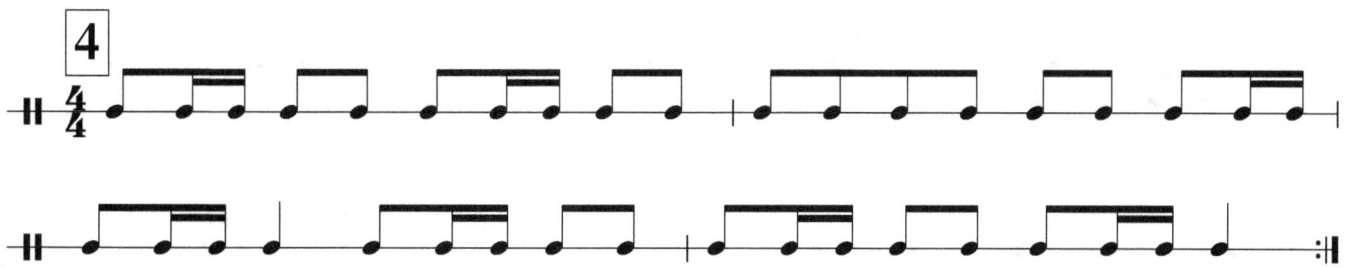

Lesson 5.4

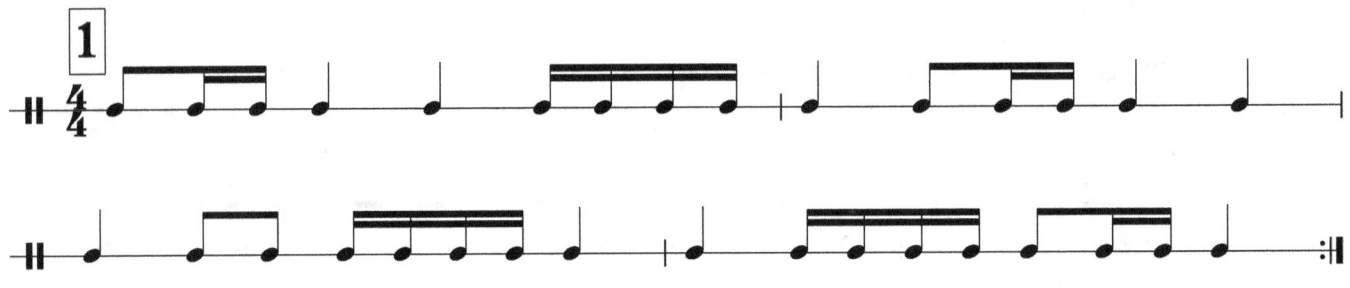

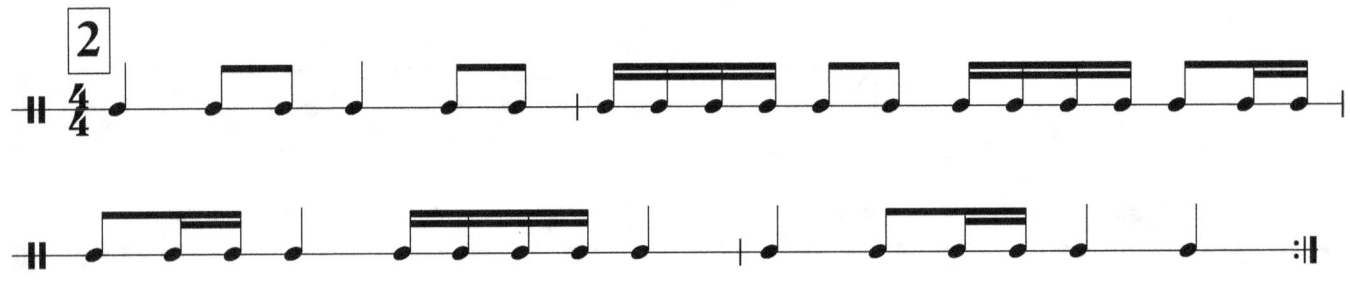

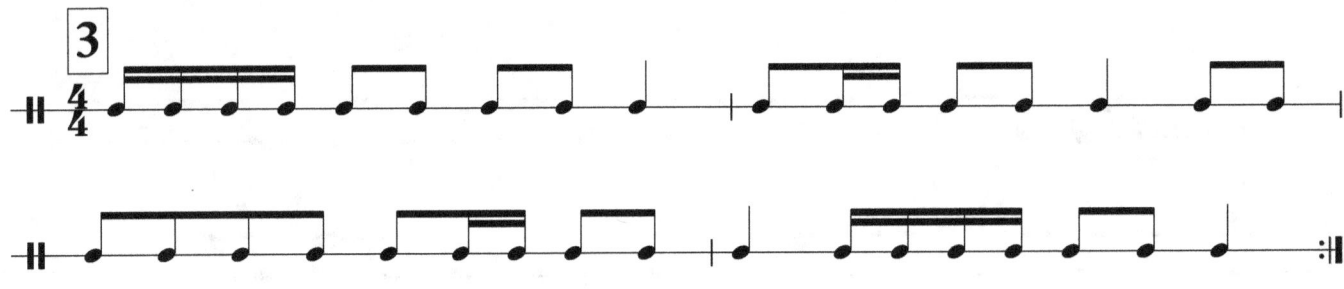

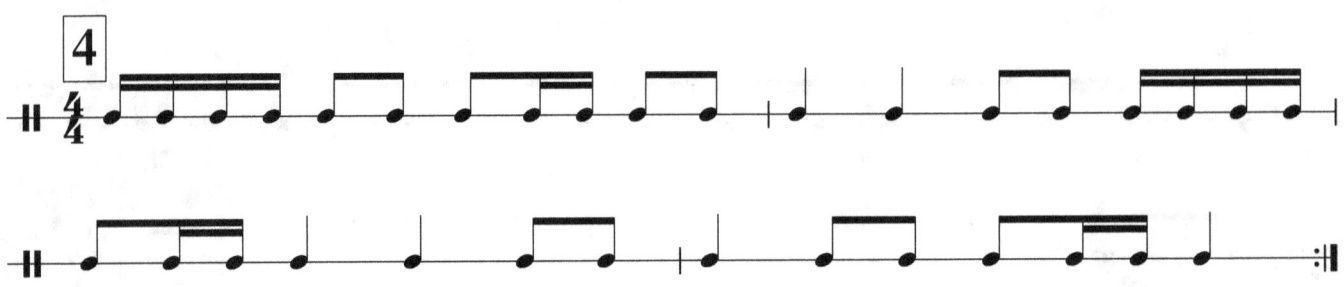

Lesson 5.5

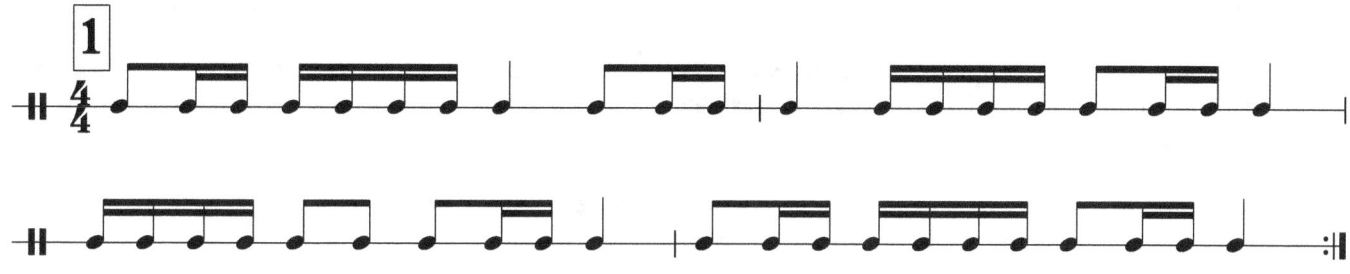

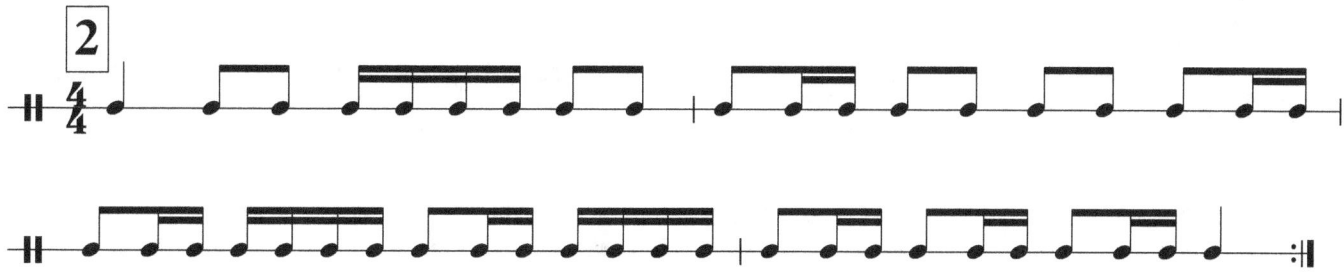

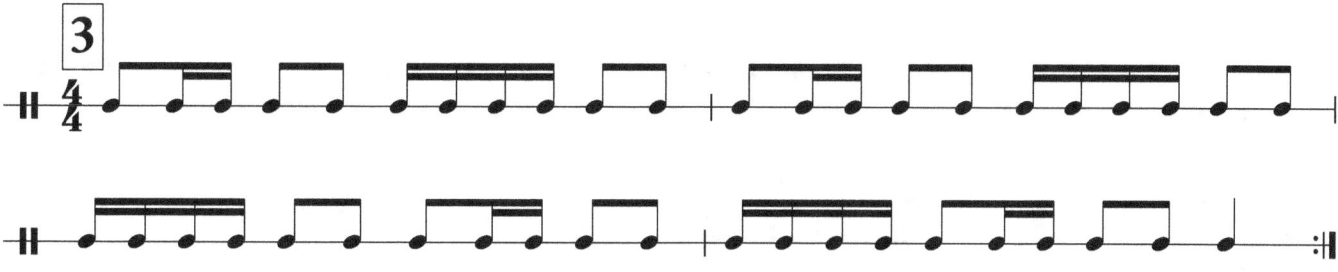

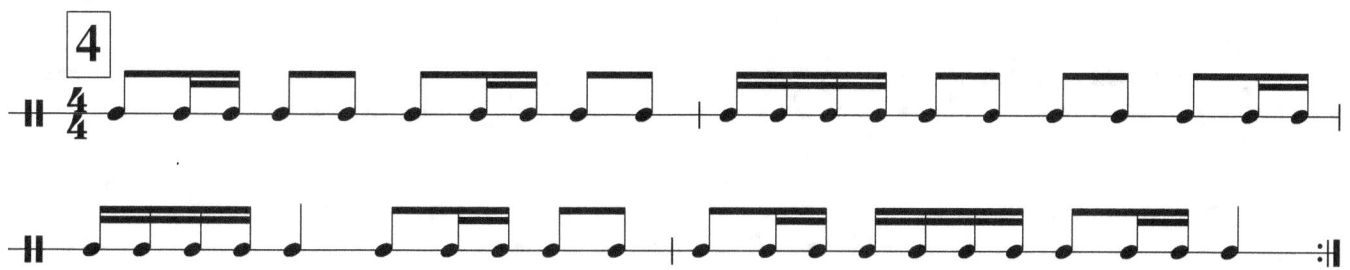

Lesson 5.6

*There is not a Play Along Track for this page! Use a metronome to keep a steady beat. Start at 80 BPM and work up to 110 BPM.

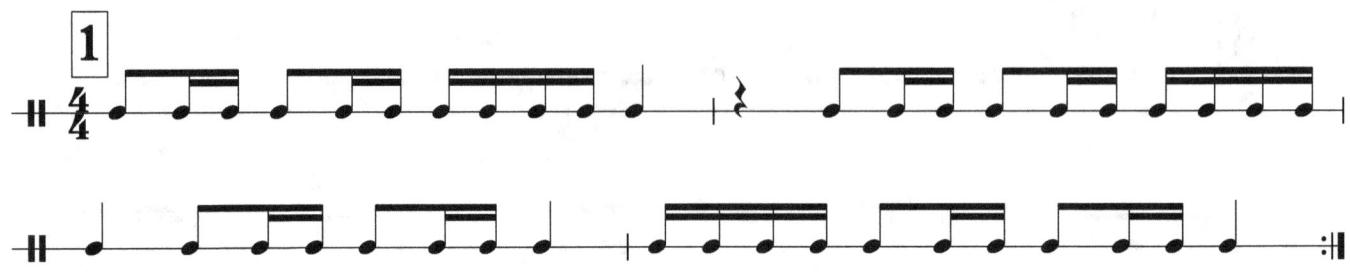

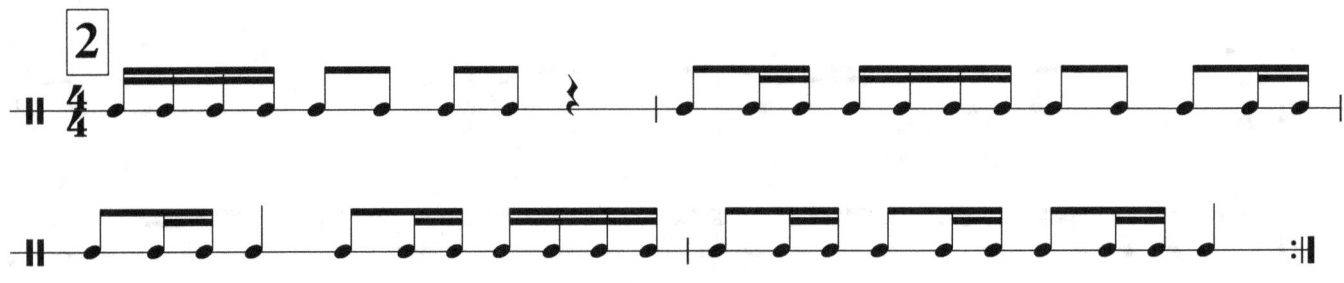

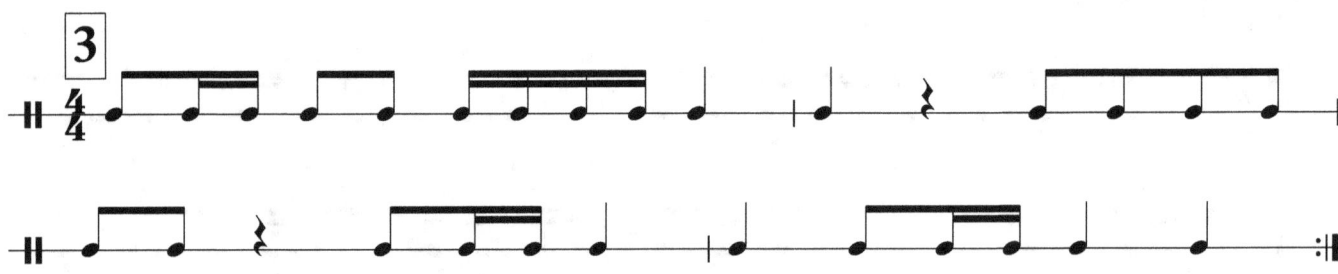

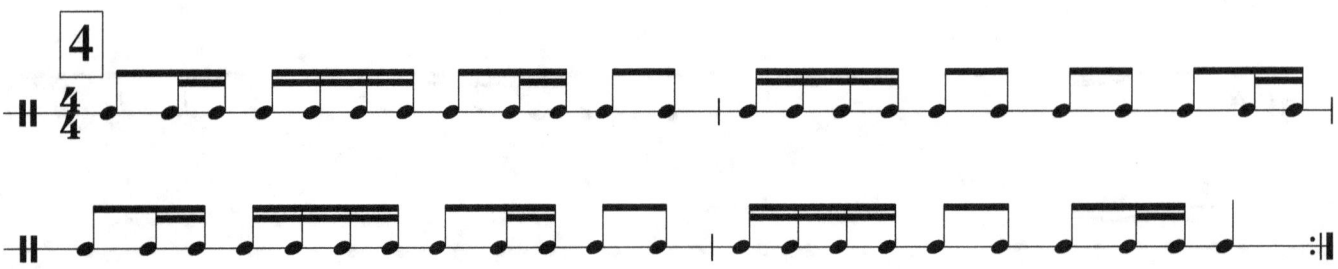

Lesson 5.7

There is not a Play Along Track for this page! Use a metronome to keep a steady beat. Start at 80 BPM and work up to 110 BPM.

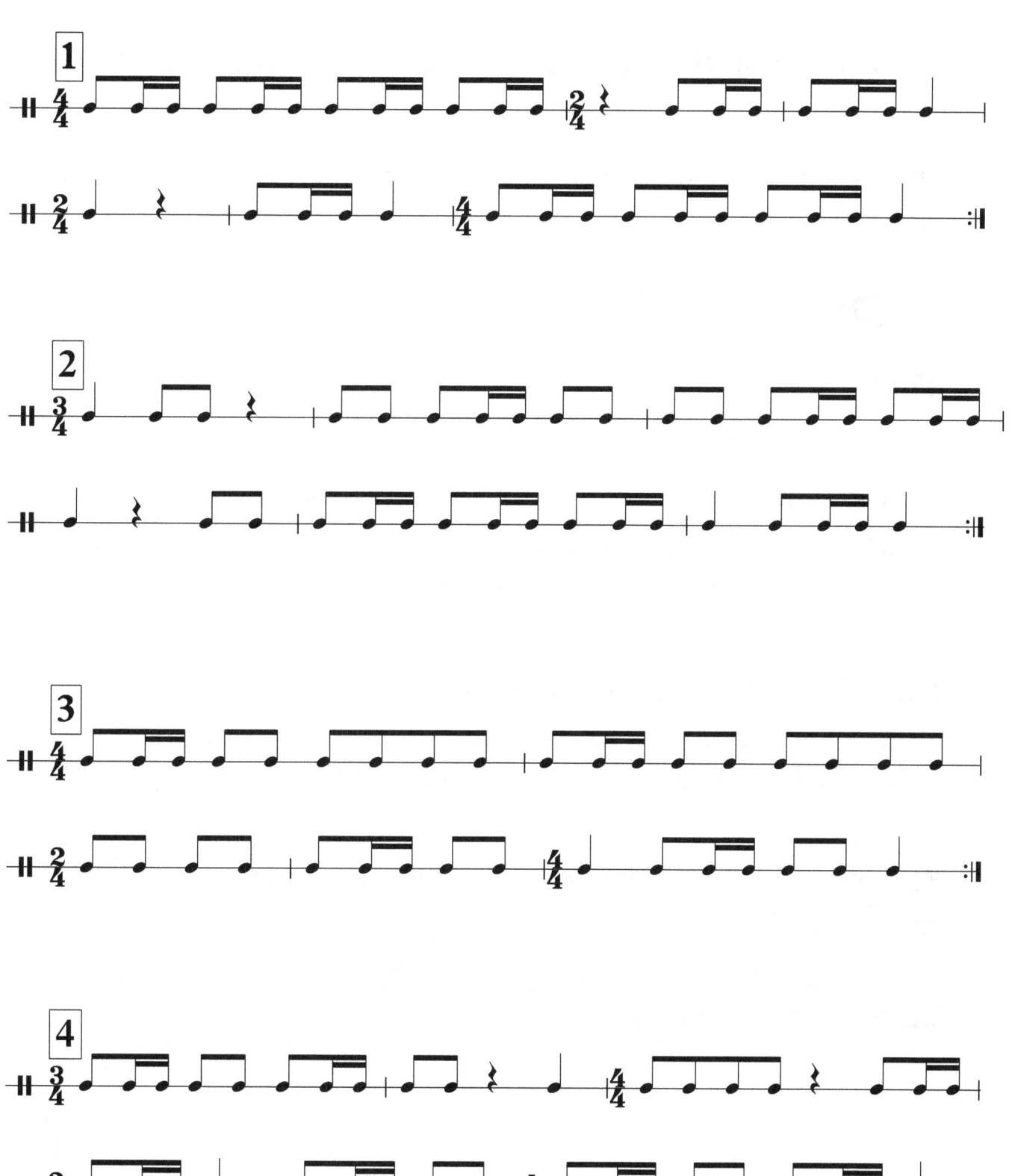

Unit 6

Sixteenth Notes and Eighth Notes Combined

This is what two sixteenth notes followed by one eighth note looks like:

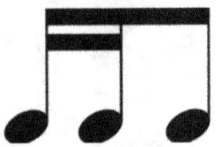

This combination takes up one beat. The two sixteenth notes take up the first half of the beat and the eighth note takes up the second half of the beat.

This is counted by giving the first sixteenth note the number of whatever beat it falls on. The second sixteenth note will always be called E, and the eighth note will be &.

For example, if this rhythm is on beat three it would be counted 3-E-&.
No matter what beat this rhythm occurs on, it is sticked the same way: R-L-R

Lesson 6.1

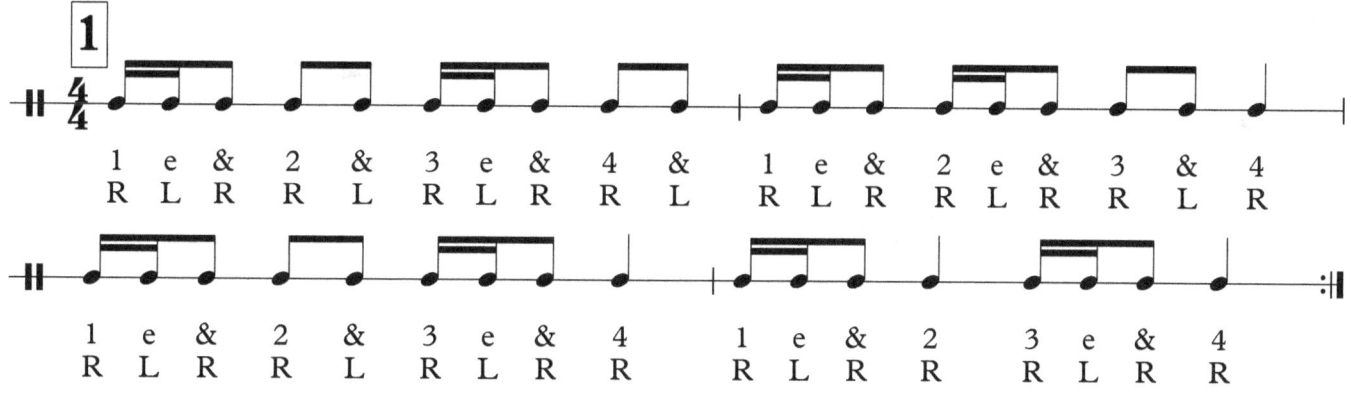

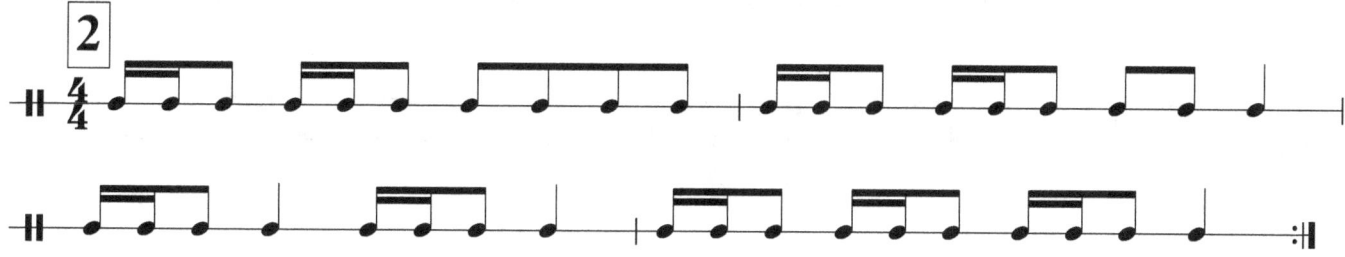

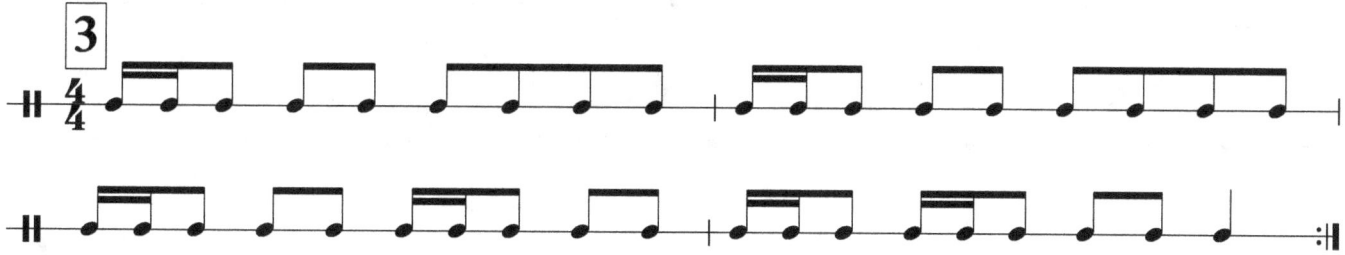

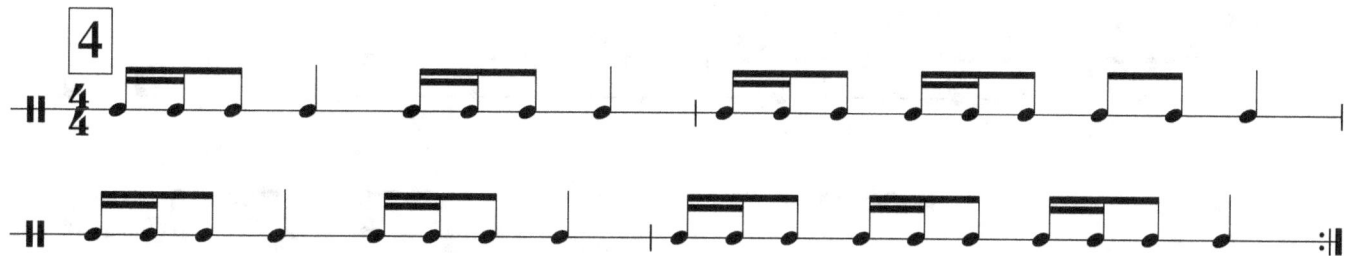

Lesson 6.2

1

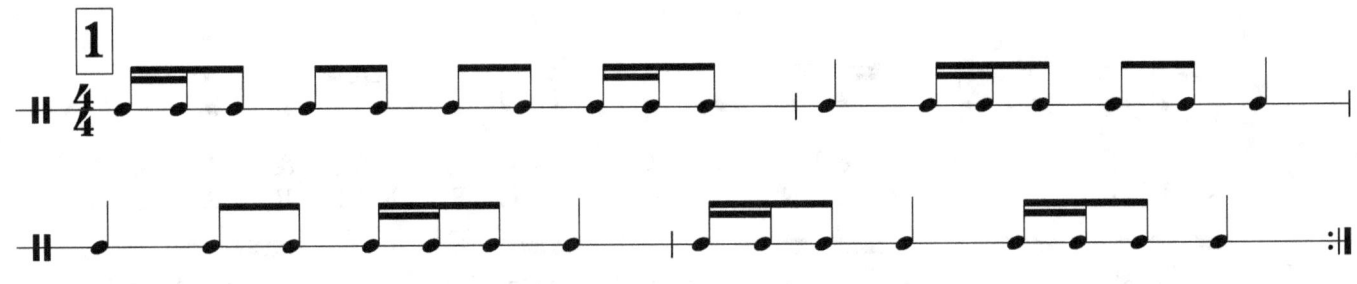

2

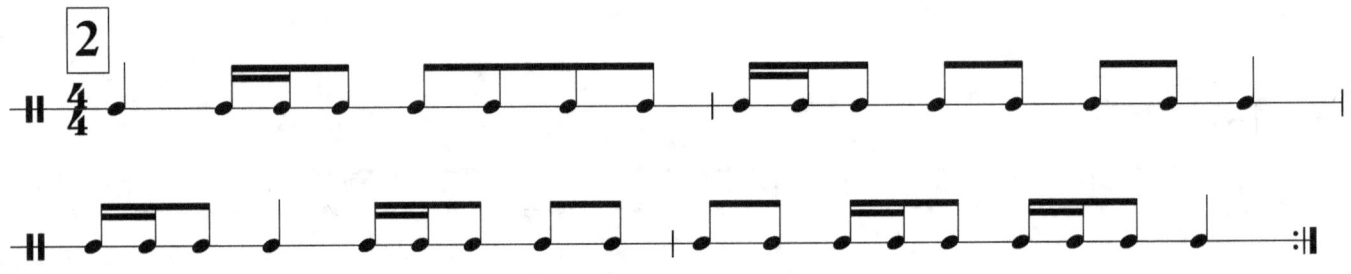

3

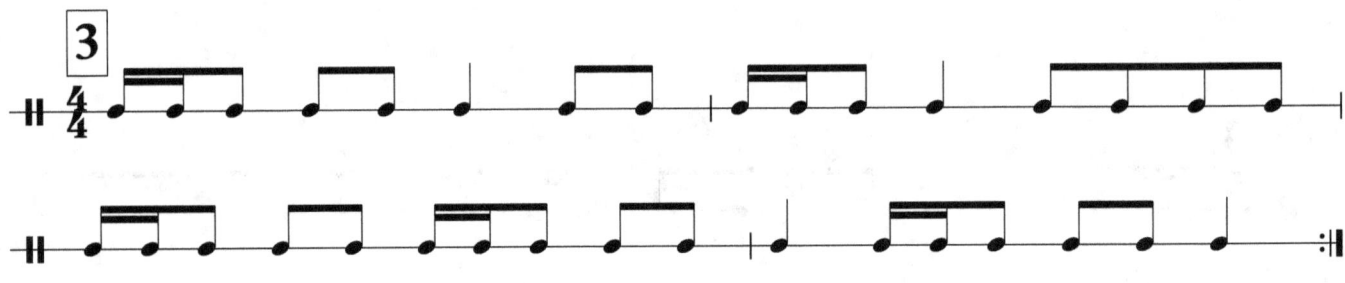

4

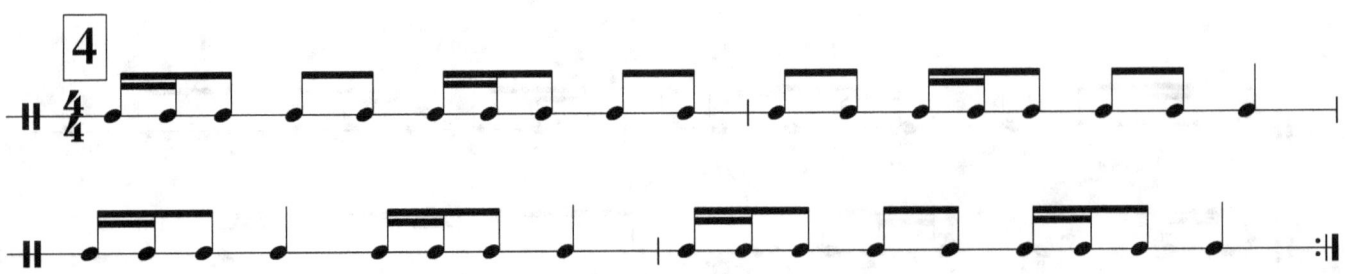

Lesson 6.3

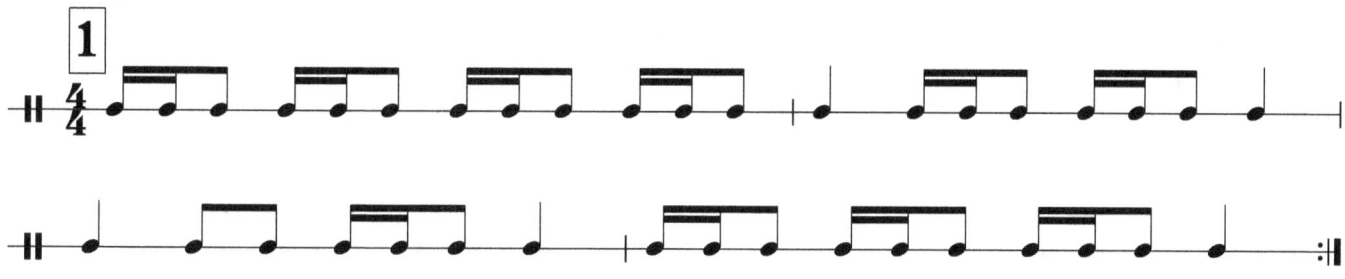

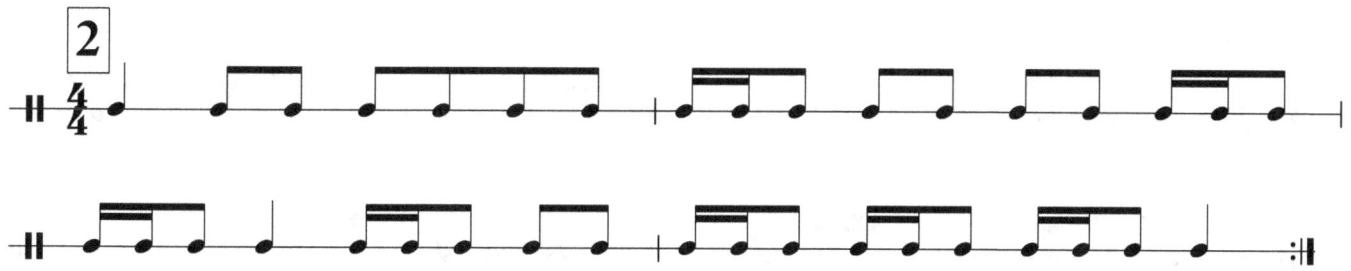

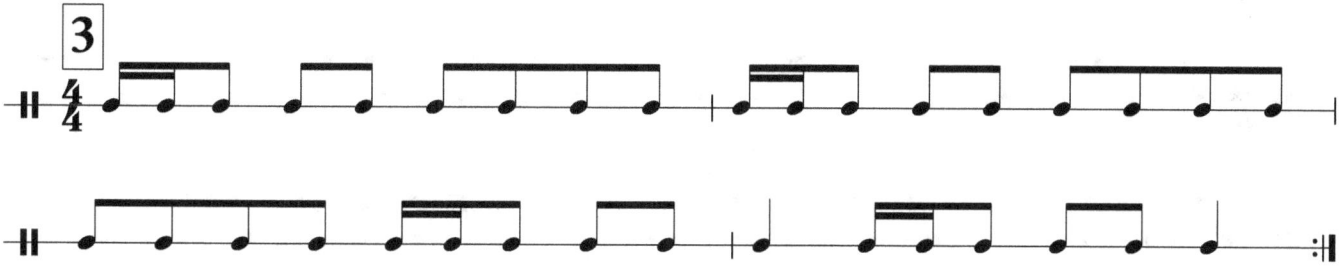

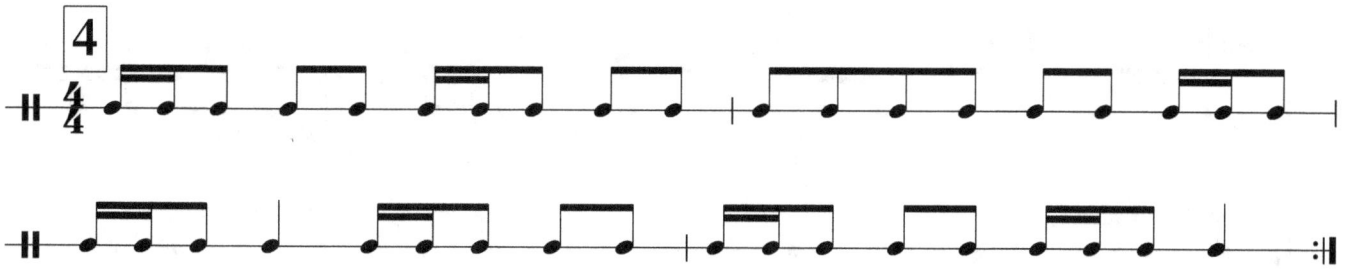

Lesson 6.4

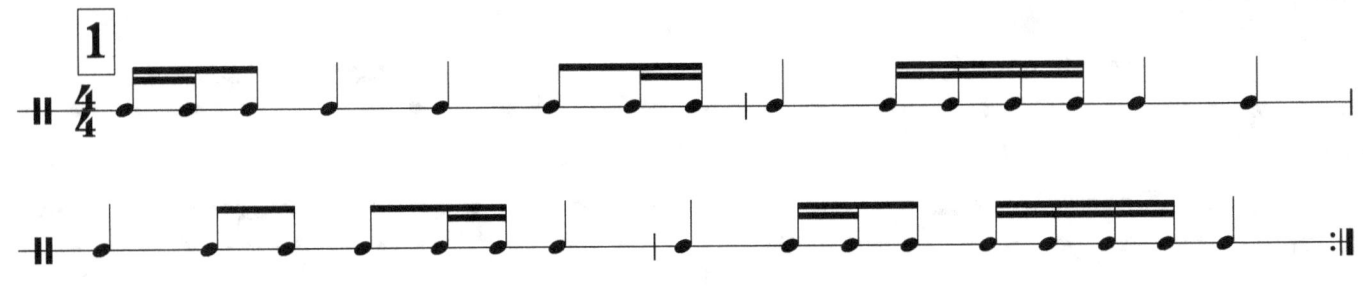

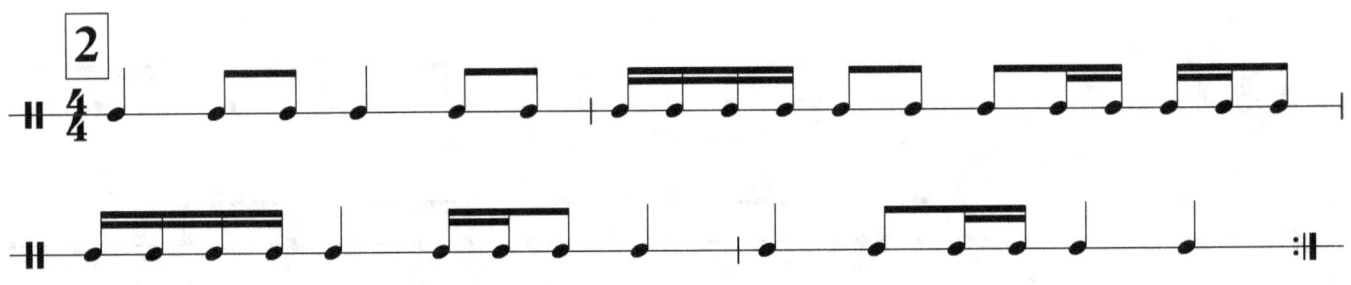

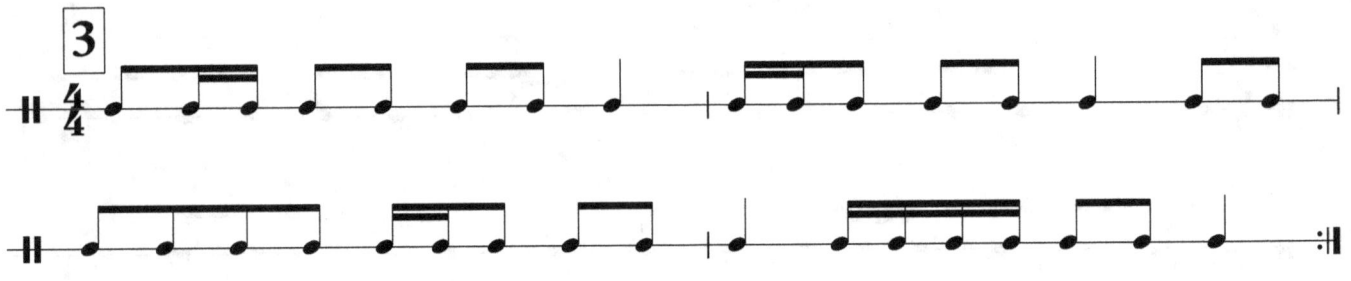

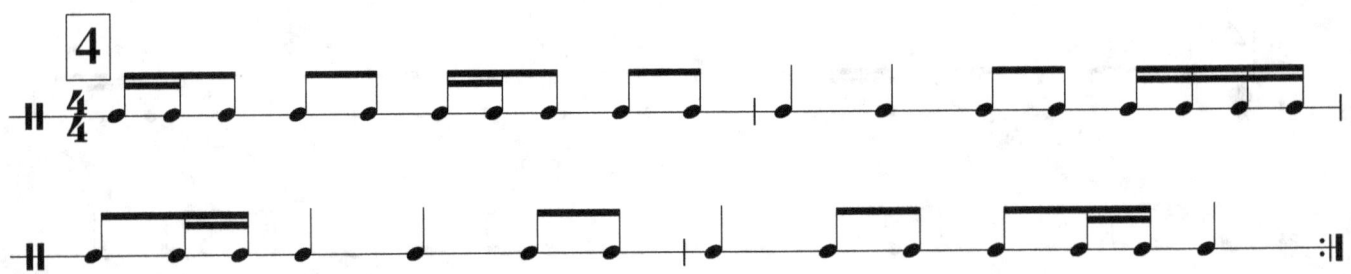

Lesson 6.5

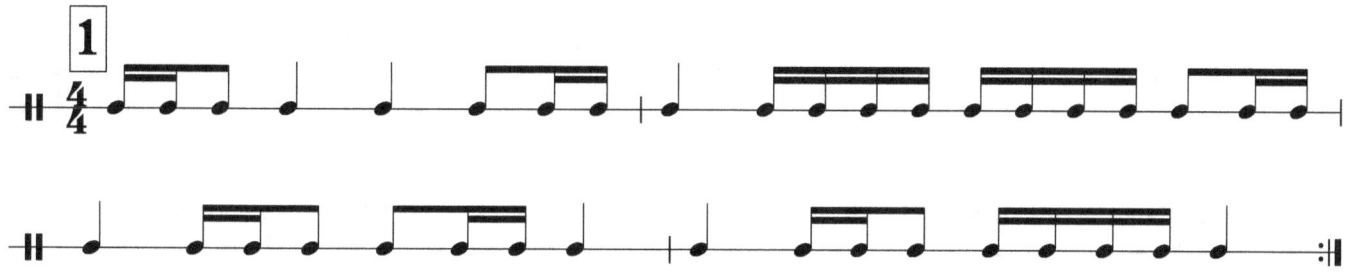

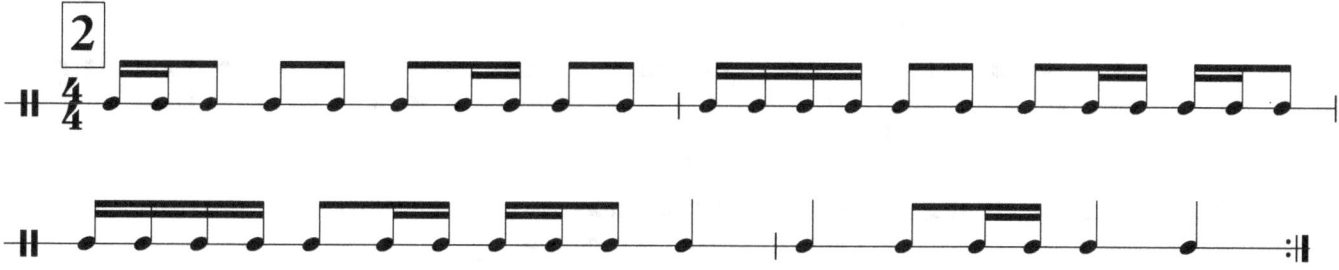

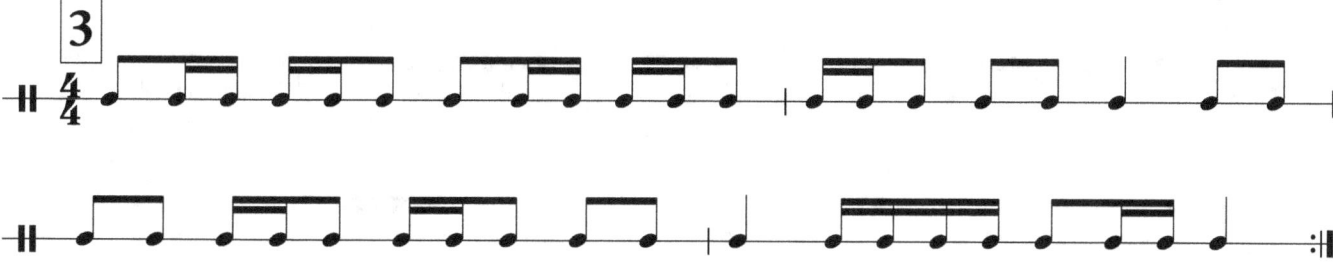

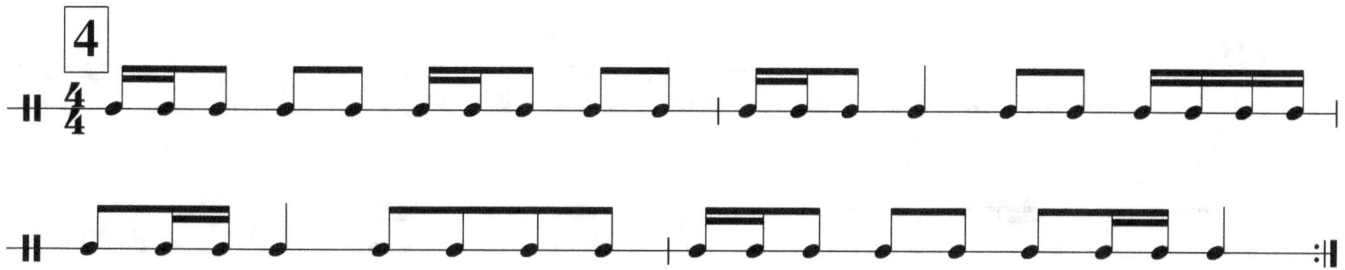

48

Lesson 6.6

*There is not a Play Along Track for this page! Use a metronome to keep a steady beat. Start at 80 BPM and work up to 110 BPM.

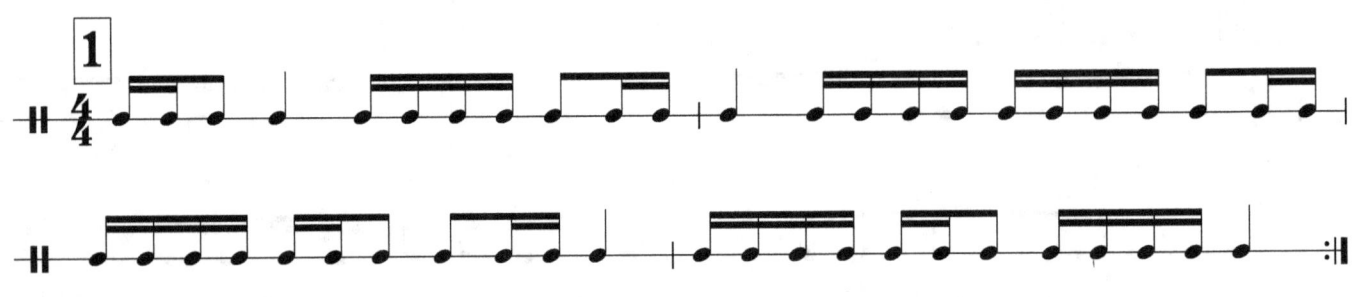

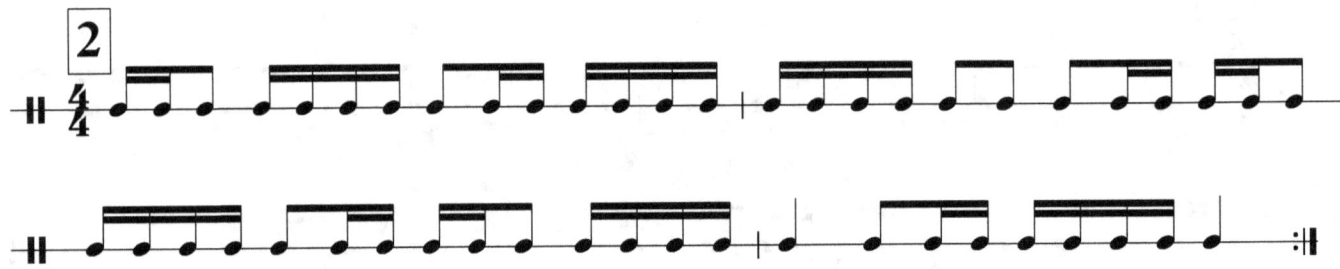

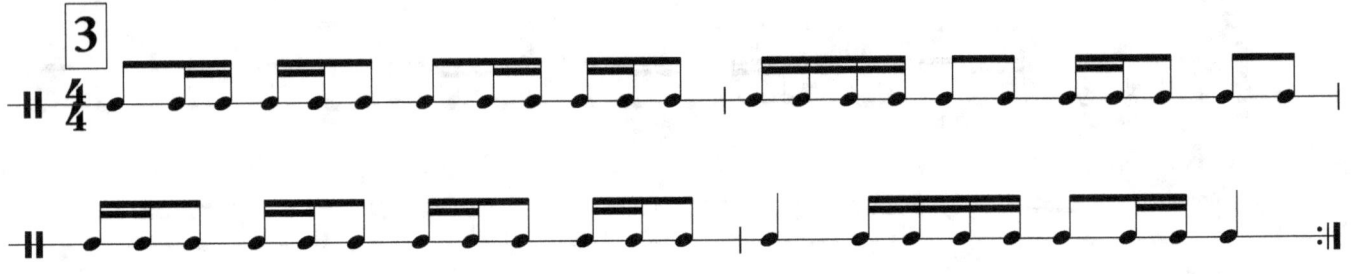

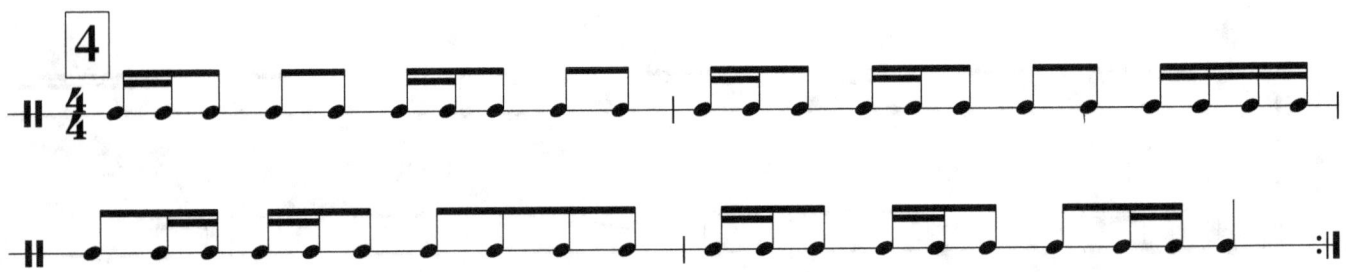

Lesson 6.7

49

*There is not a Play Along Track for this page! Use a metronome to keep a steady beat. Start at 80 BPM and work up to 110 BPM.

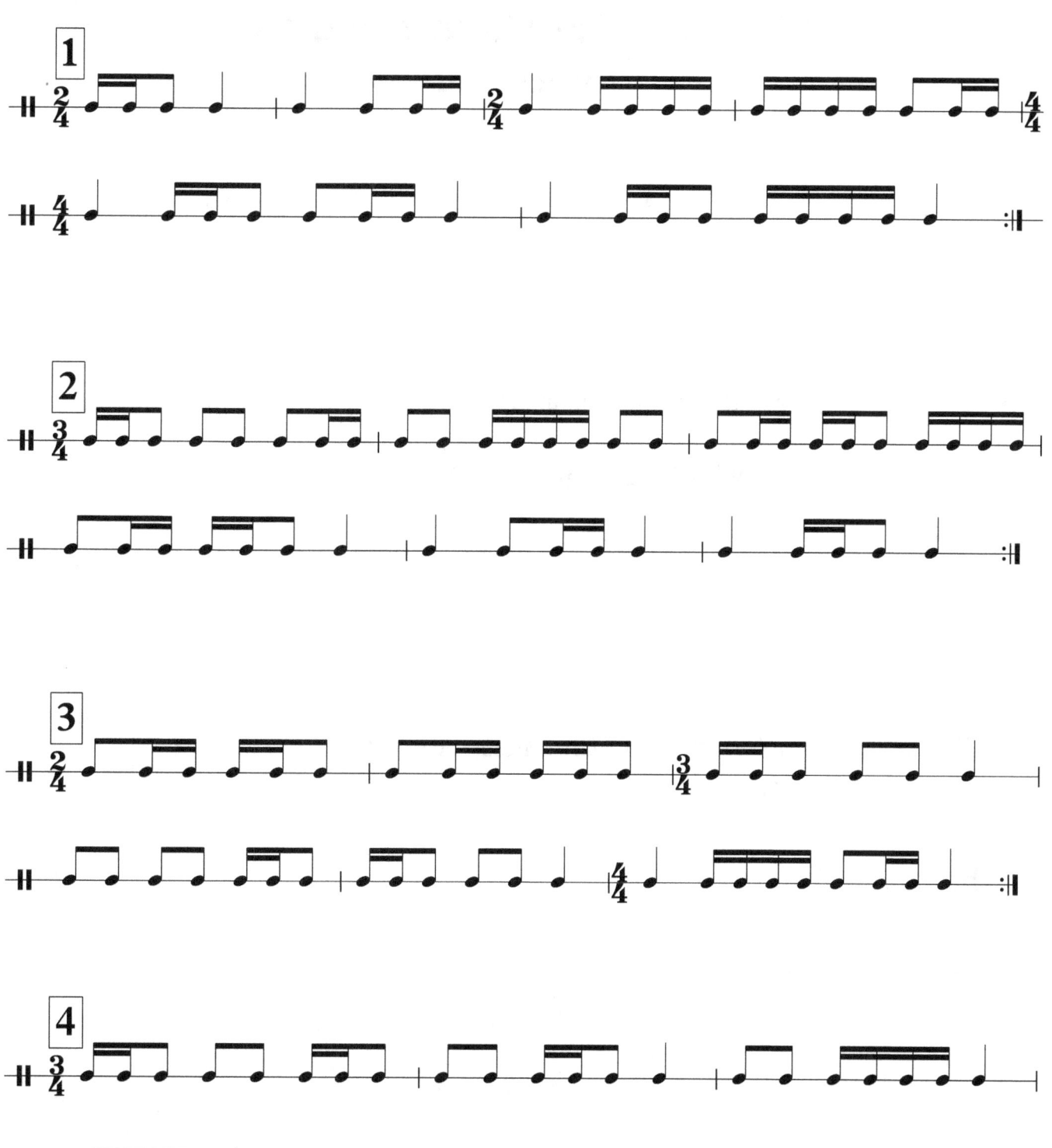

Unit 7

The Multiple Bounce Roll
"Buzz Roll"

Remember these letters –   **P.L.A.D.**

- **P**(inch) – Give a slight pinch at your Fulcrum.

- **L**(ow) – Approach the multiple bounce roll from a low stick height.

- **A**(rm) – Arm should be the primary driving force for the stroke.

- **D**(rop) – Drop you back 3 fingers SLIGHTLY off the stick.

Watch this video on how to create a good multiple bounce stroke:

https://safeYouTube.net/w/y2Hp

The Multiple Bounce Roll Cont.

This is a Quarter Note Roll: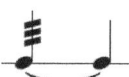

The three slashes will indicate that a multiple bounce roll should be played. The curved line under the two quarter notes is a tie. The tie indicates that the sound of the roll should connect to the quarter note.

Use a sixteenth note hand motion for the multiple bounce rolls.

When playing a roll, first determine how many sixteenth notes "fit" in that note. You already know that a quarter note takes up one count. You also know that it takes four sixteenth notes to make one full count. The above notation will be performed as follows:

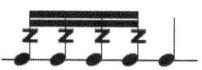 Four good multiple bounce strokes followed by a rebound stroke release.

Lesson 7.1

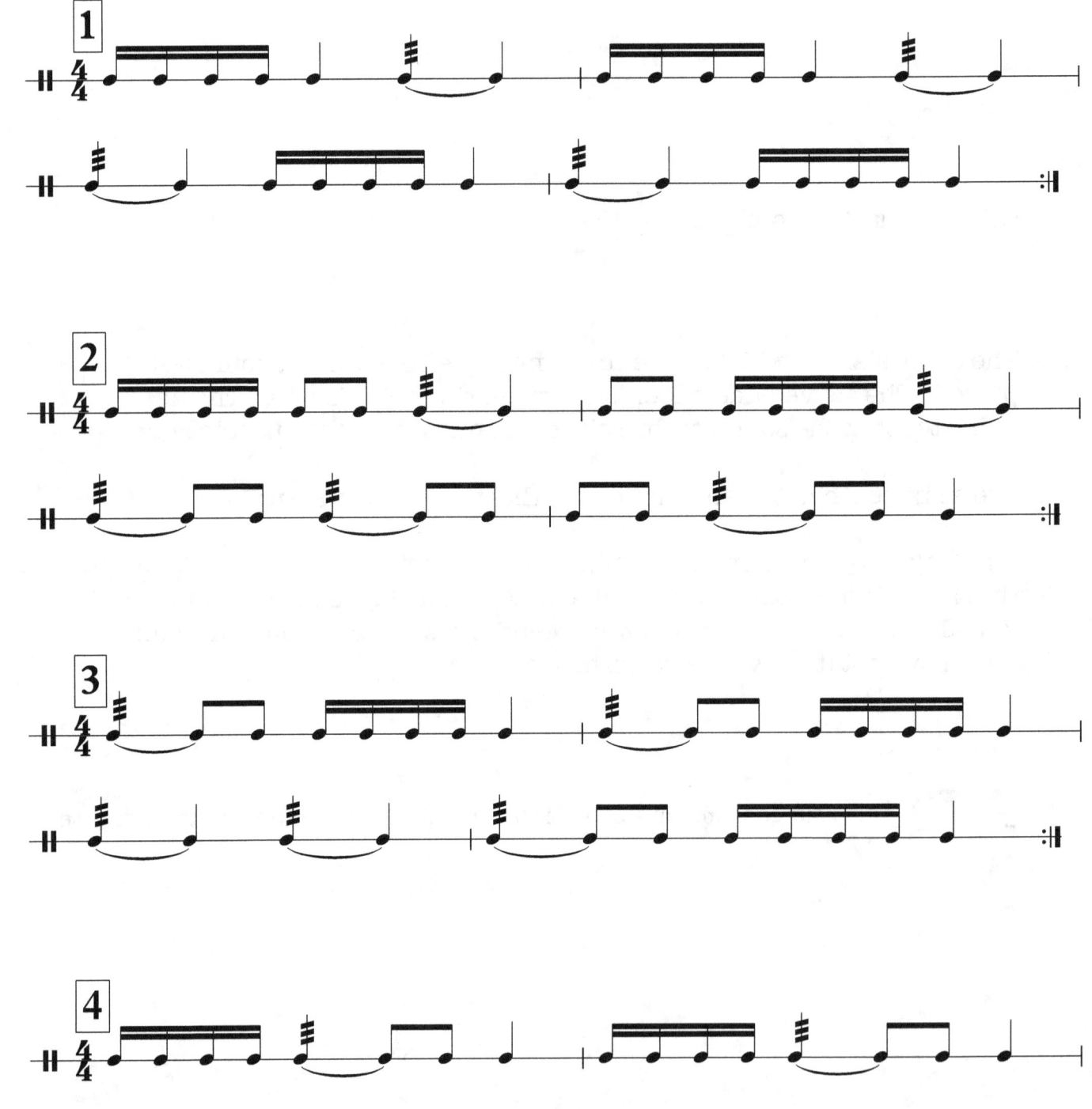

Lesson 7.2

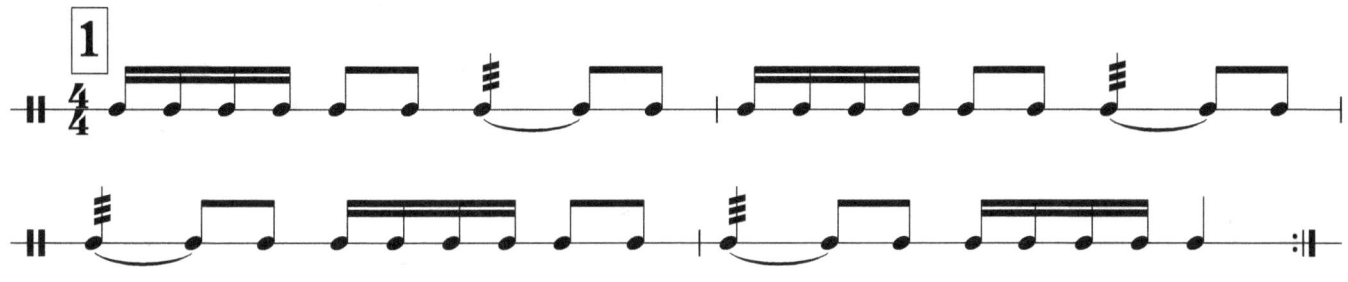

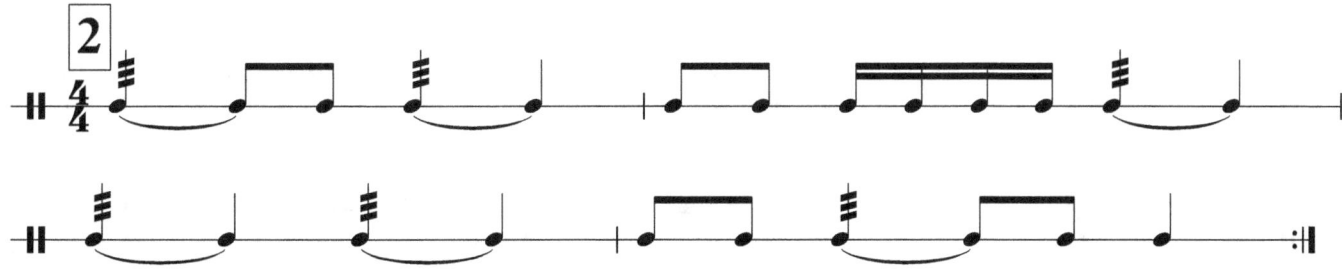

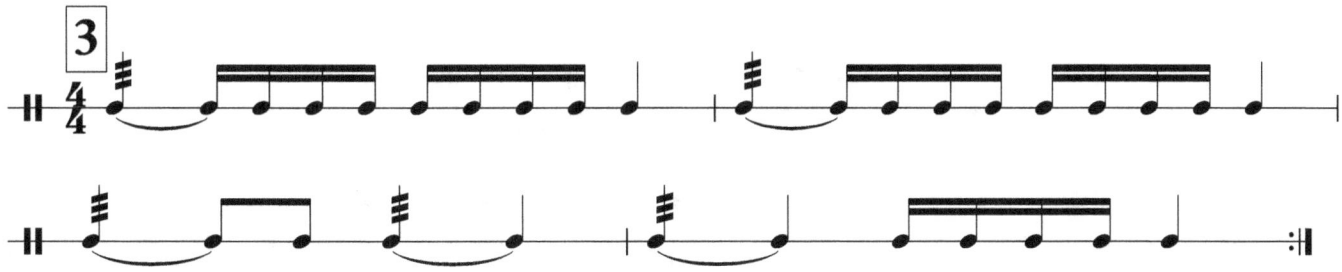

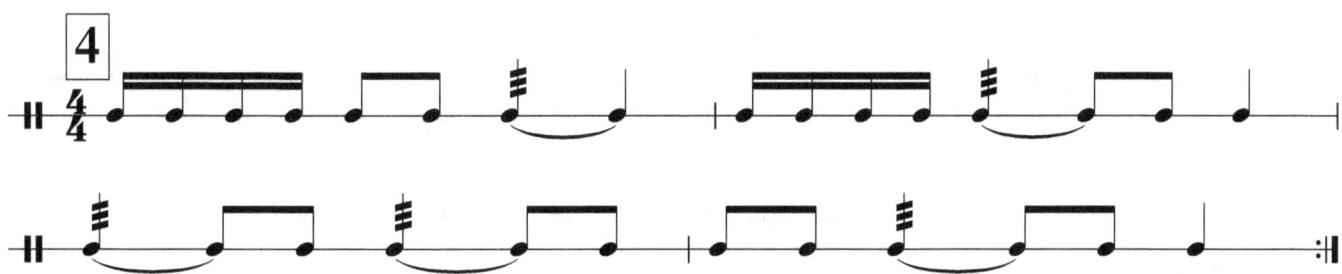

Lesson 7.3

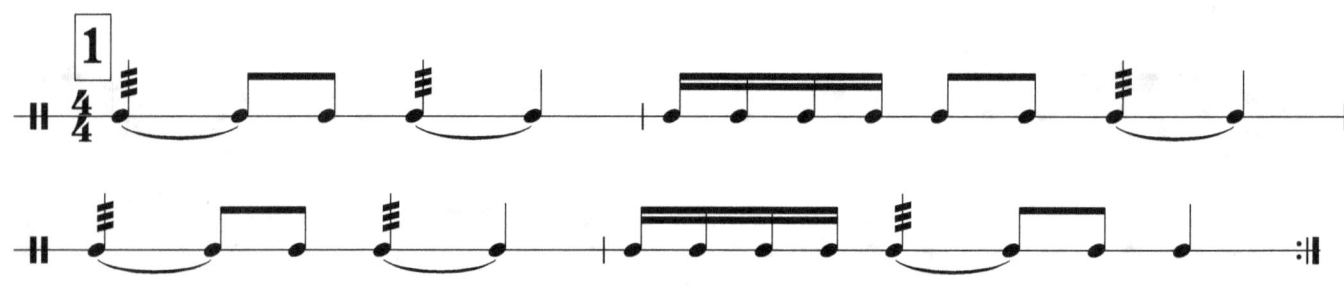

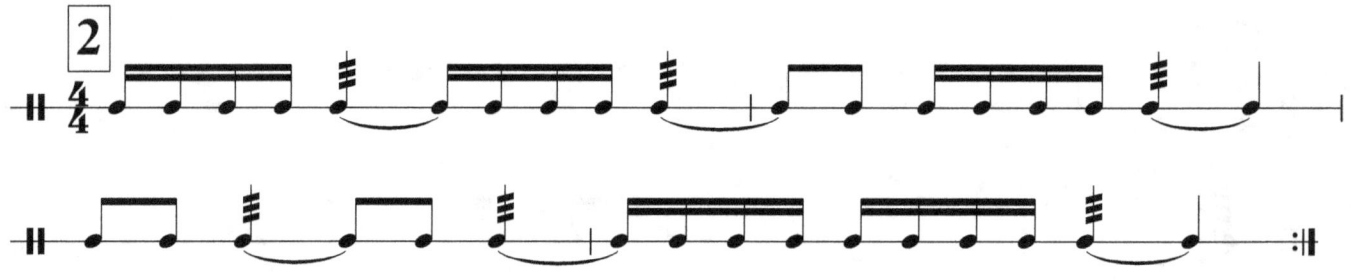

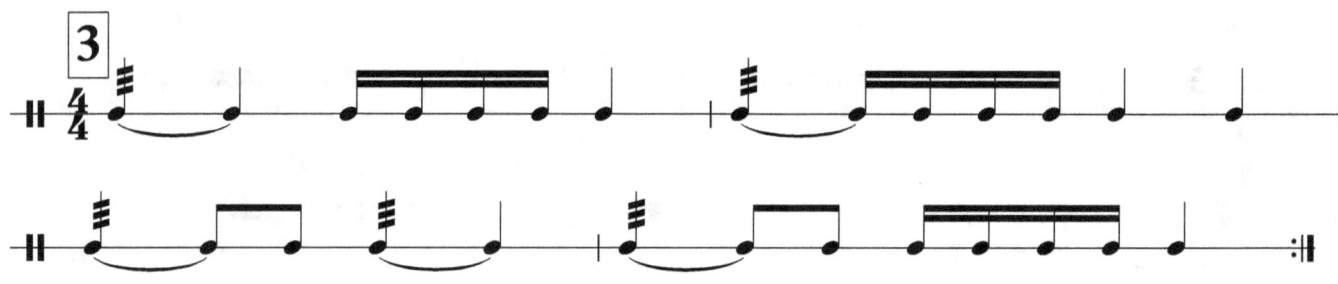

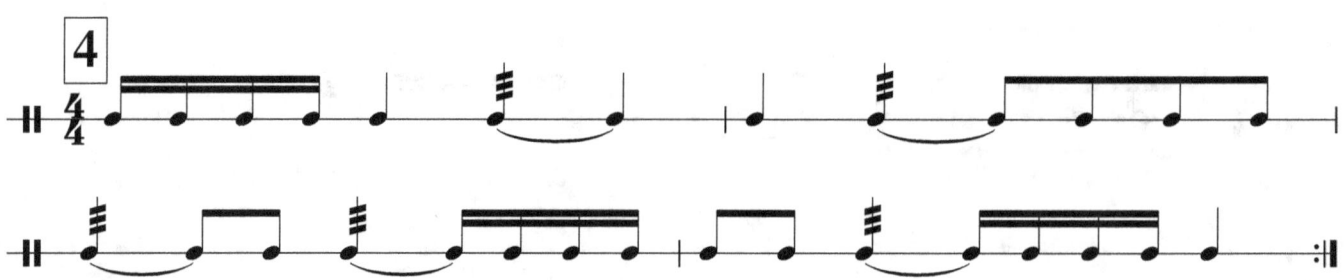

Lesson 7.4

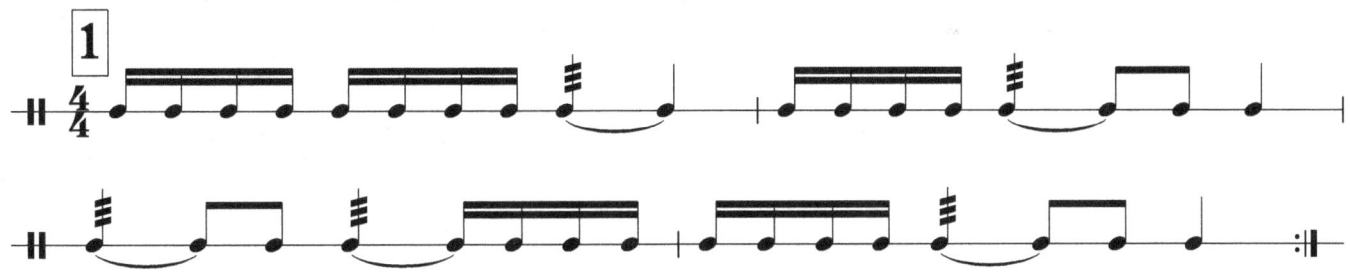

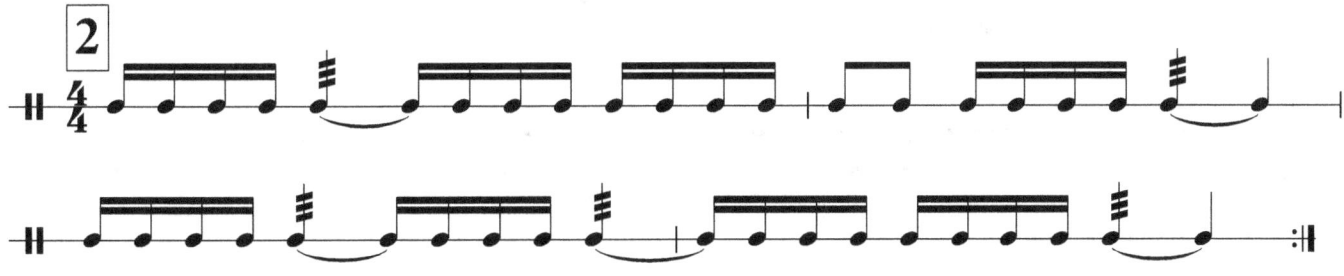

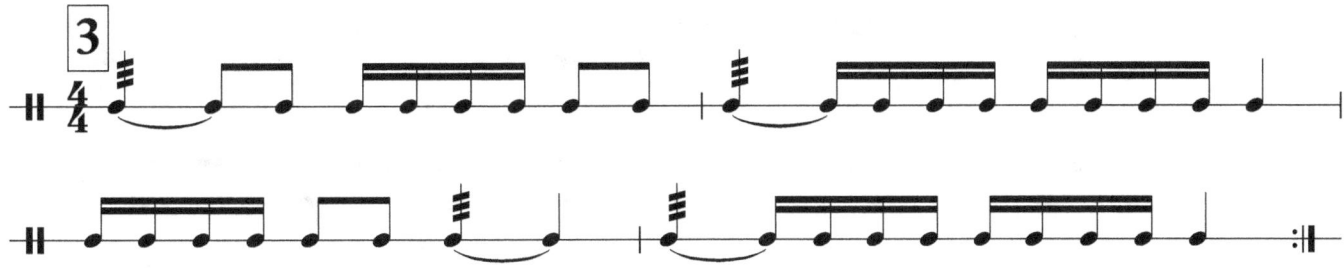

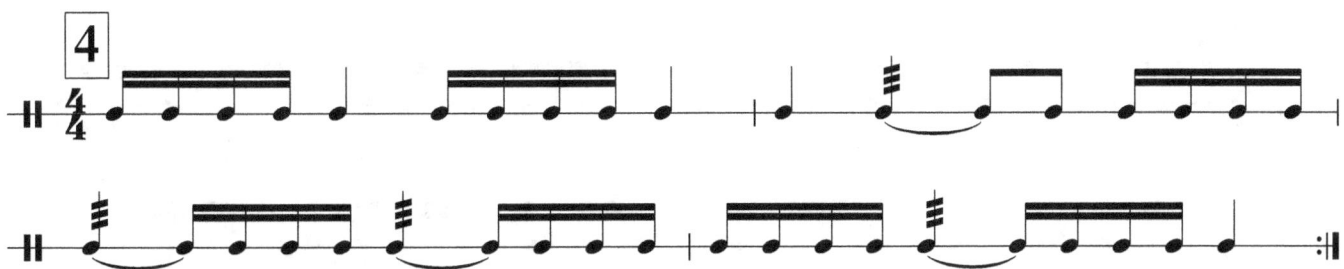

Lesson 7.5

Rhythm Review

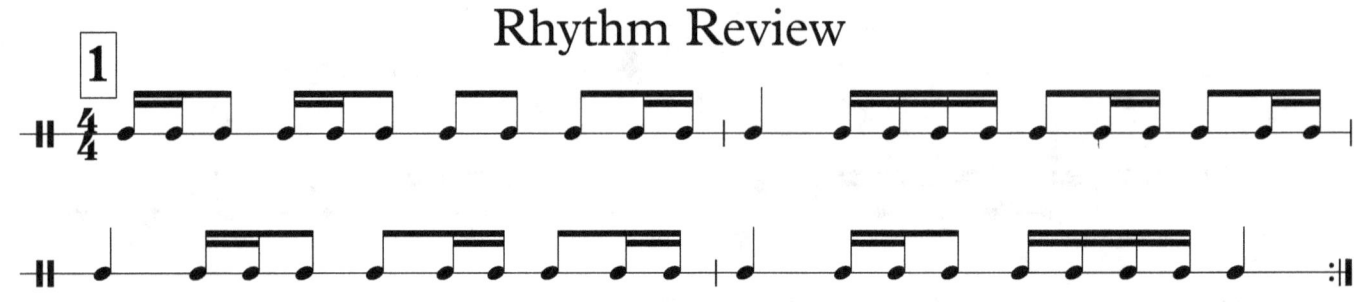

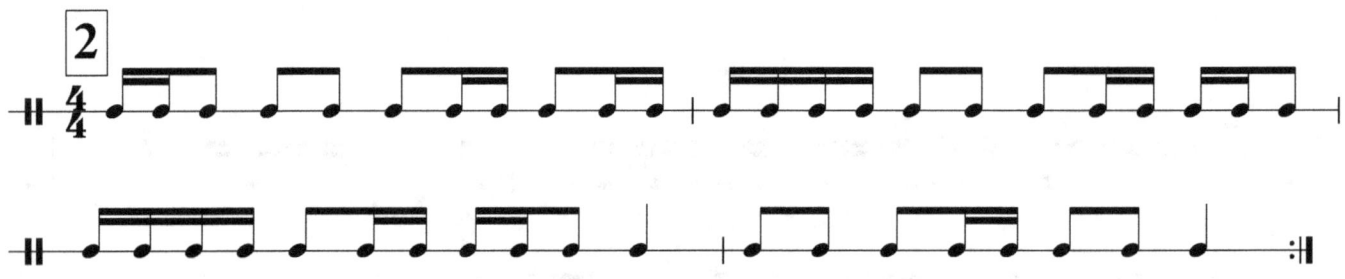

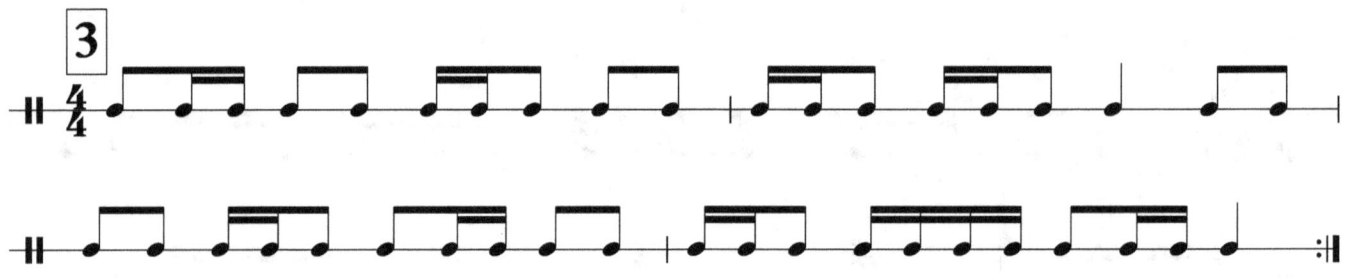

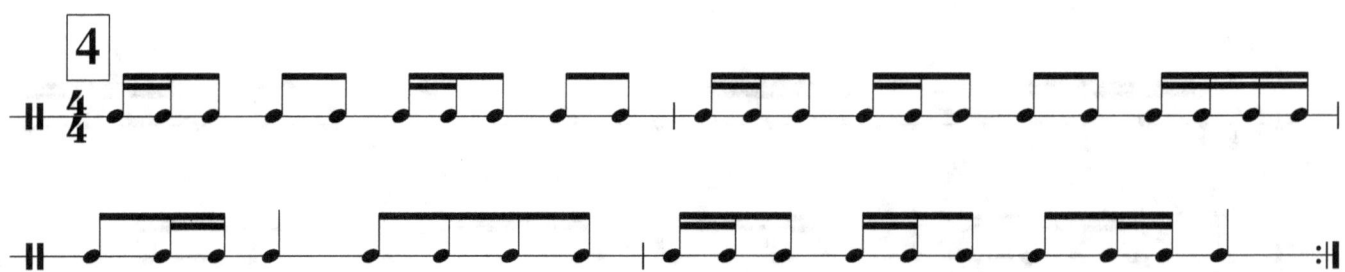

Unit 8

The Multiple Bounce Roll -

Eighth Note Rolls

Eighth Note Rolls can occur on the beat or on the &.

Before beginning this unit, review unit 5 and 6. Use the same sticking and counting to perform the rhythms in this unit.

The rolls will be notated like this:

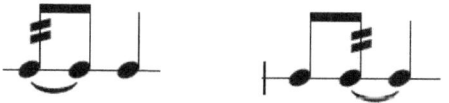

The rolls will be performed like this:

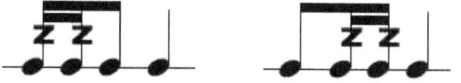

Lesson 8.1

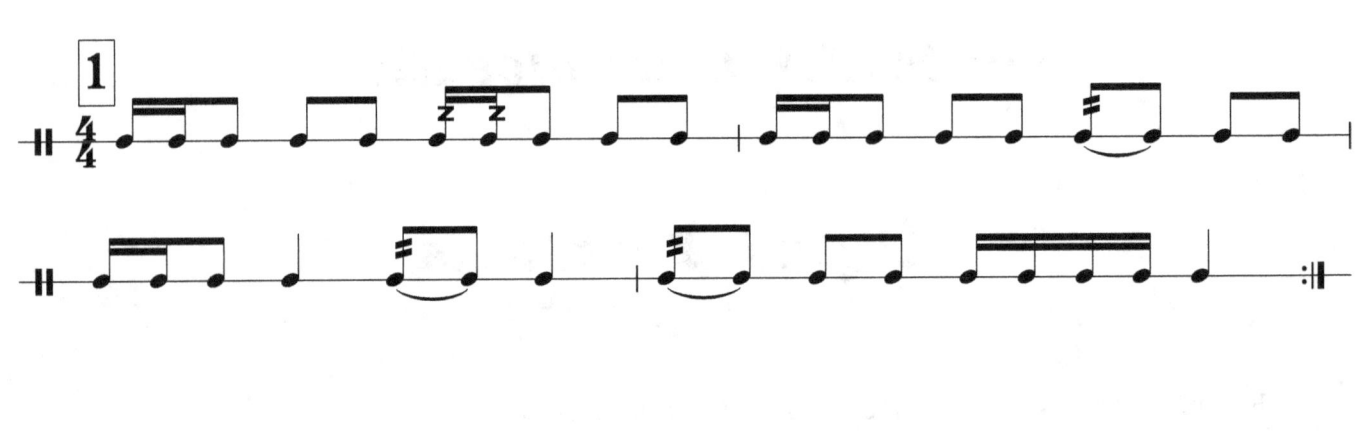

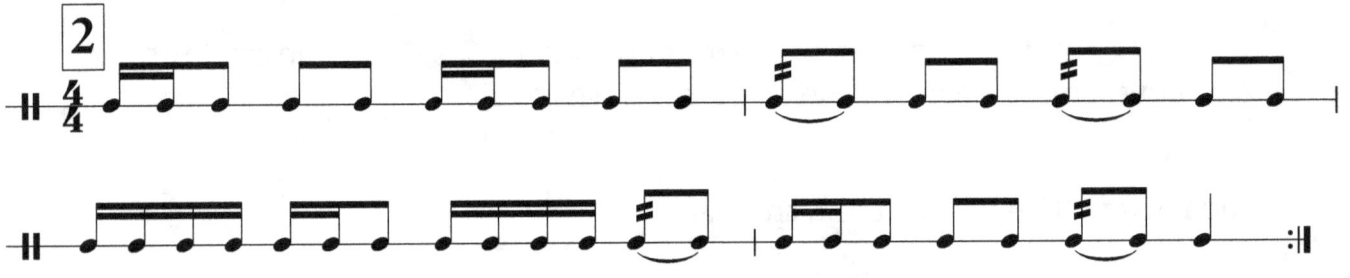

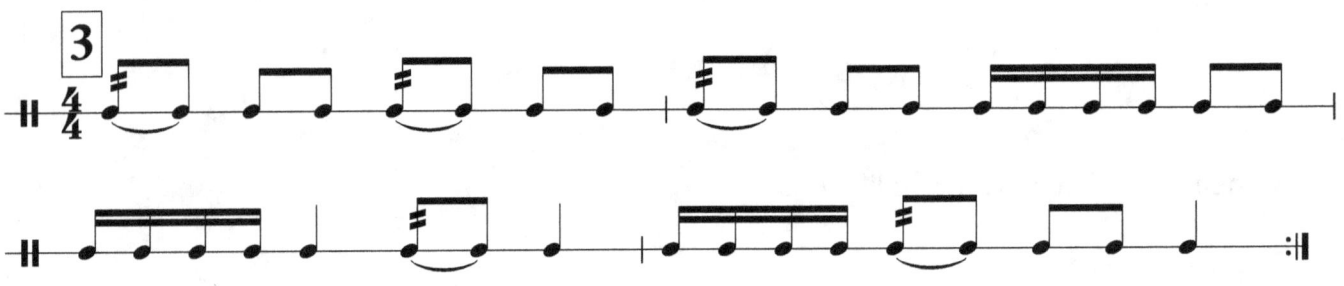

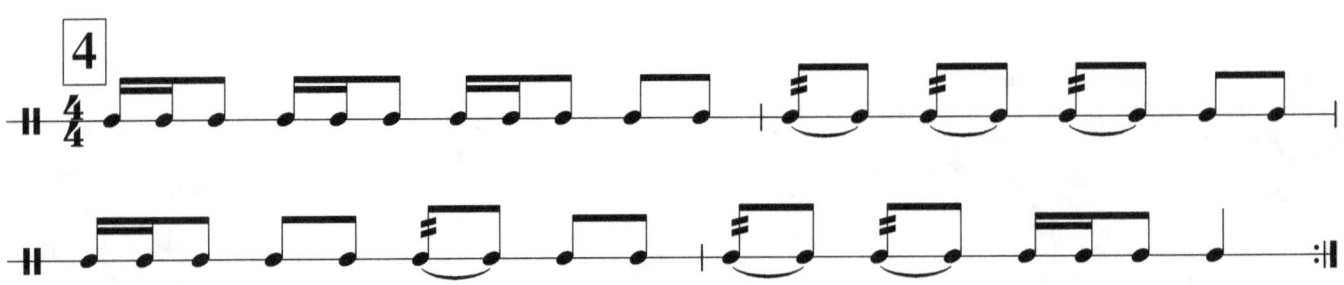

Lesson 8.2

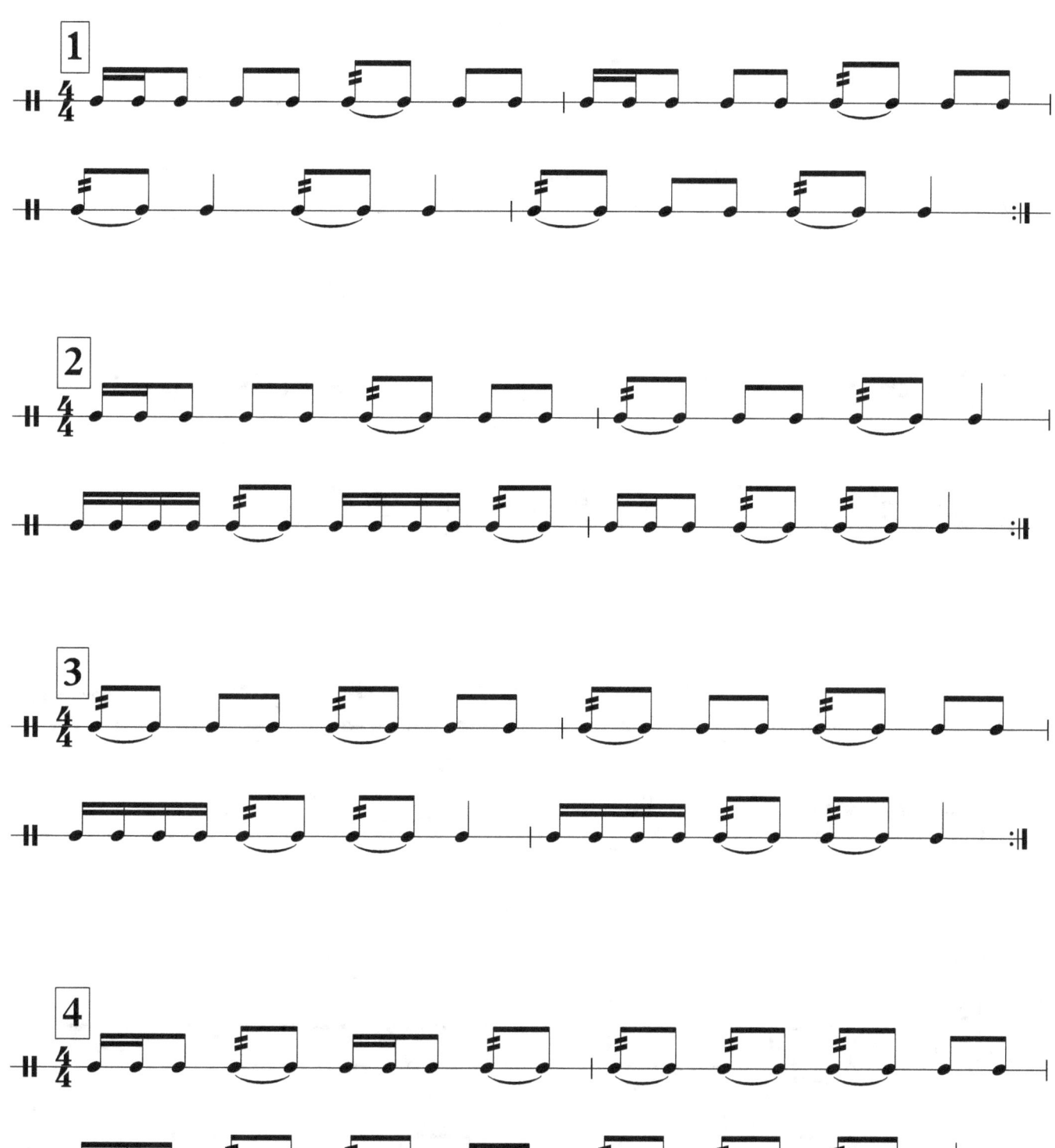

Lesson 8.3

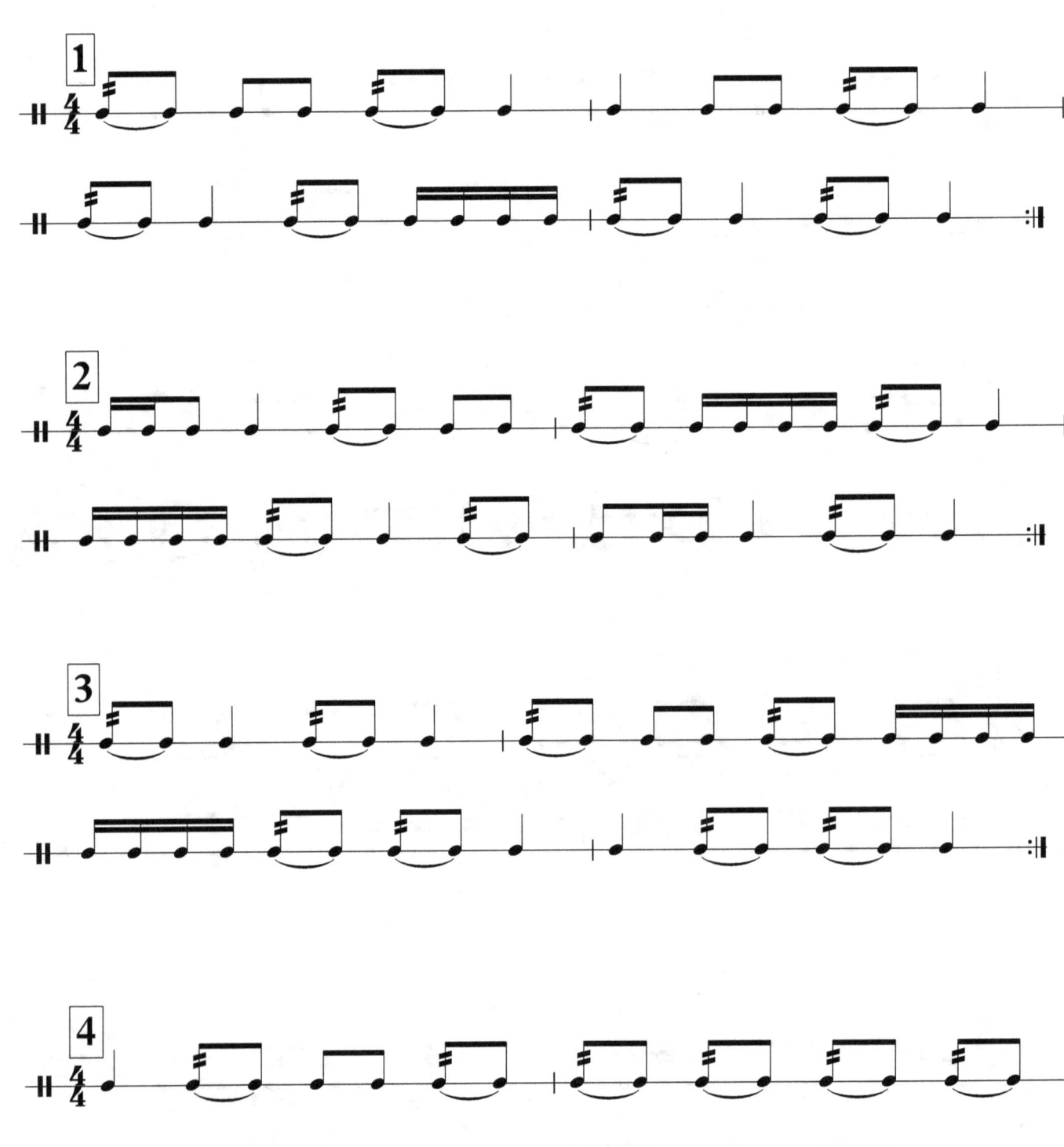

Lesson 8.4

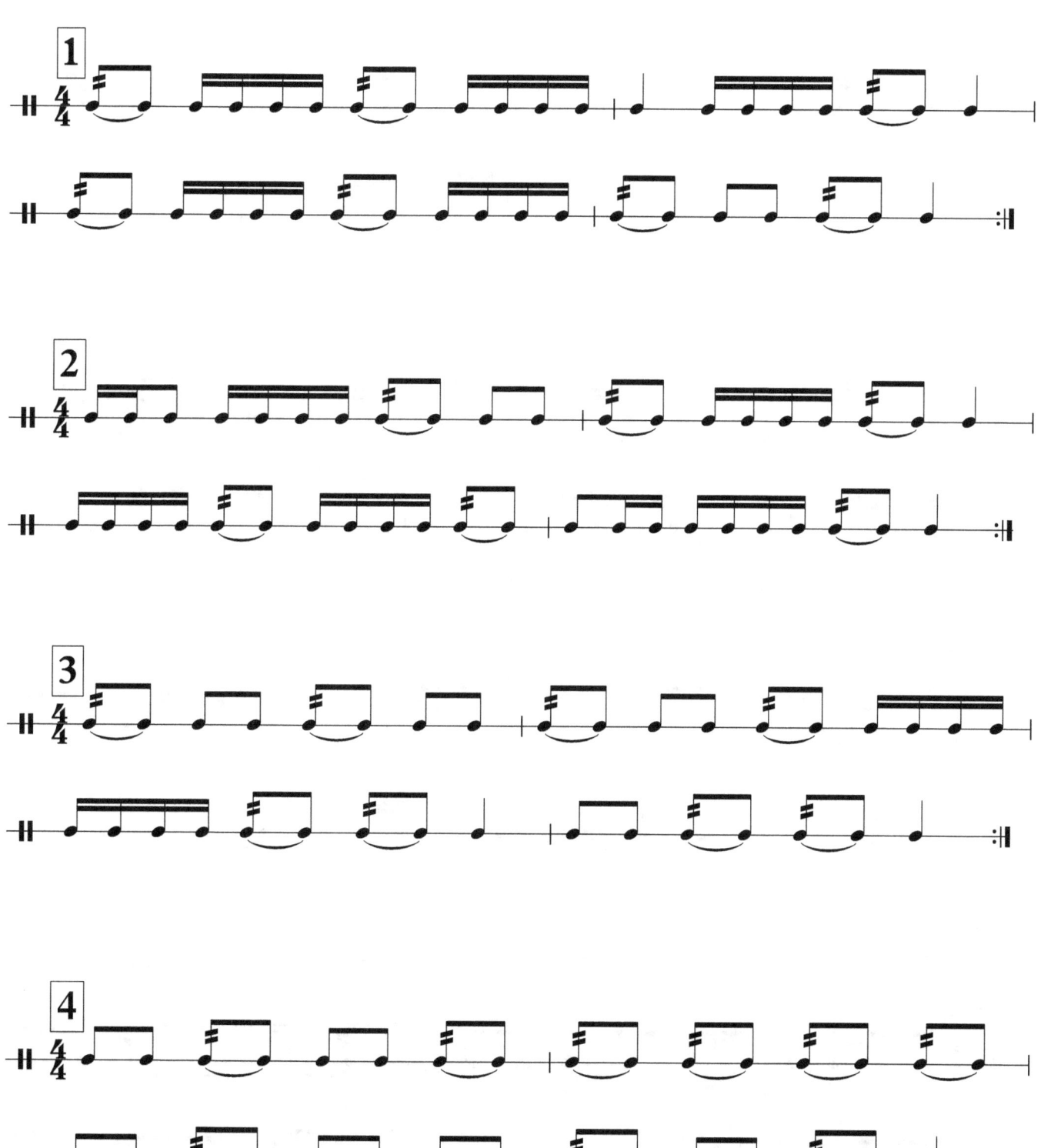

Lesson 8.5

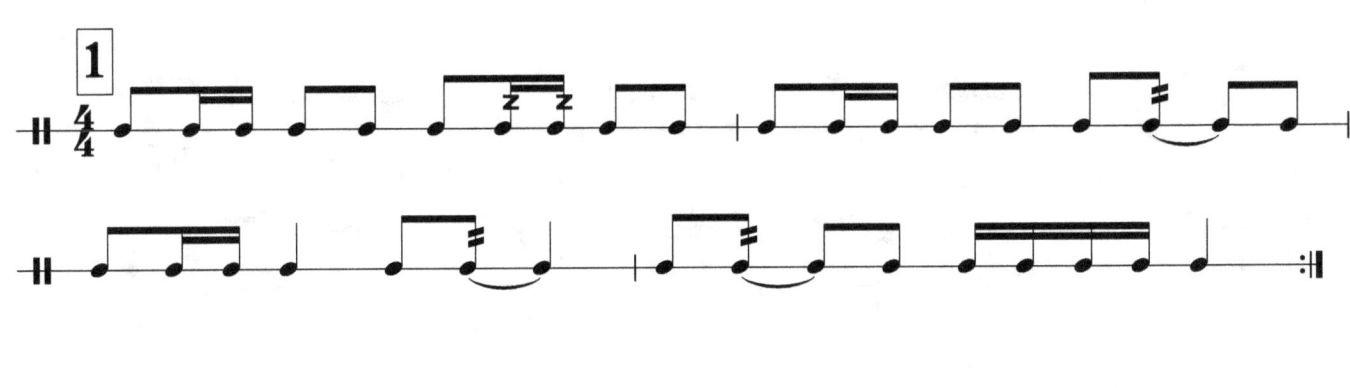

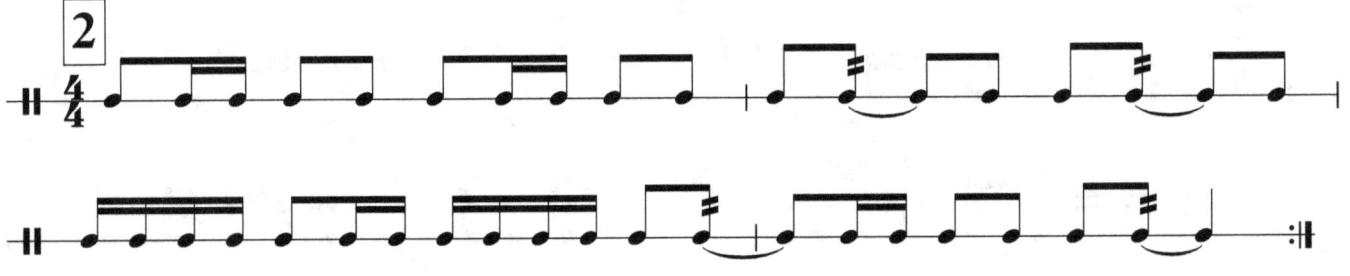

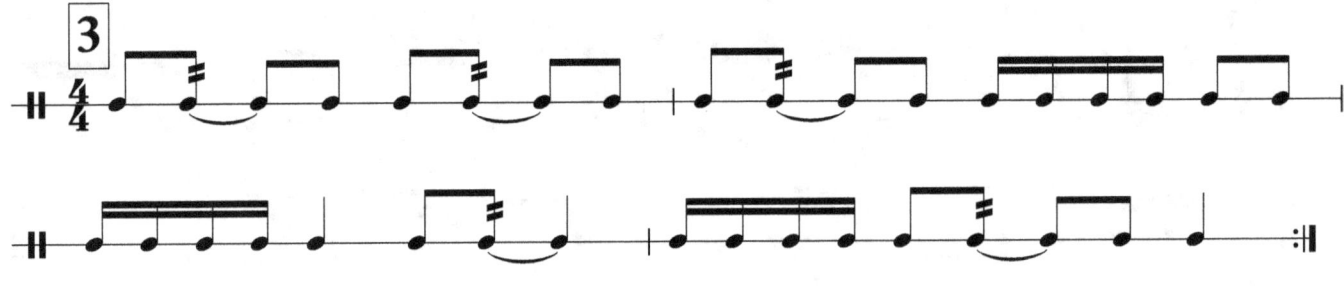

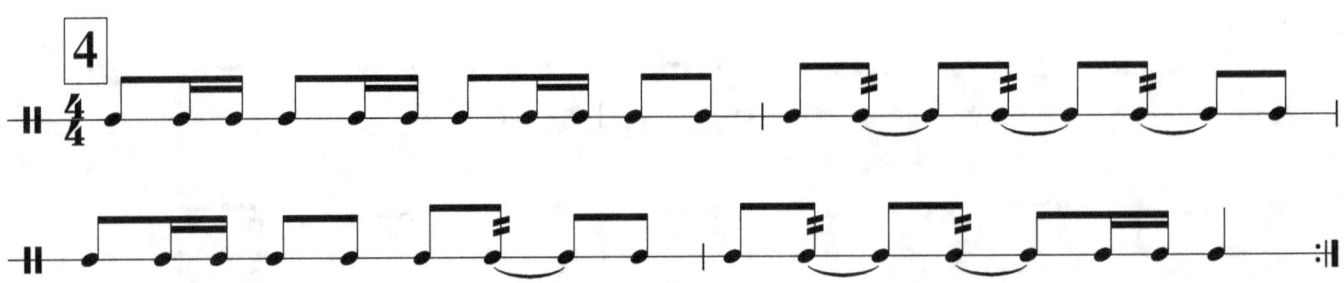

Lesson 8.6

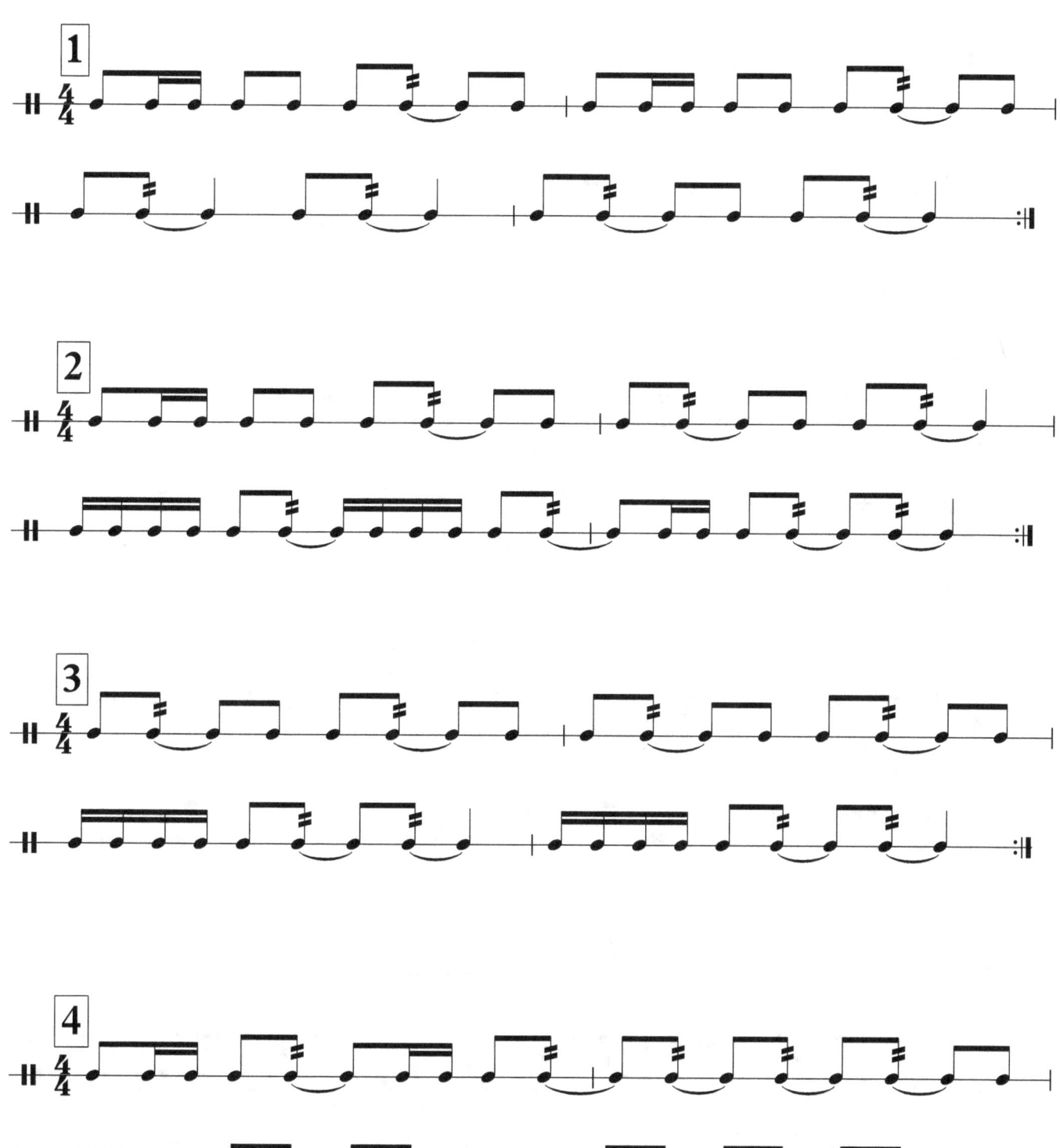

Lesson 8.7

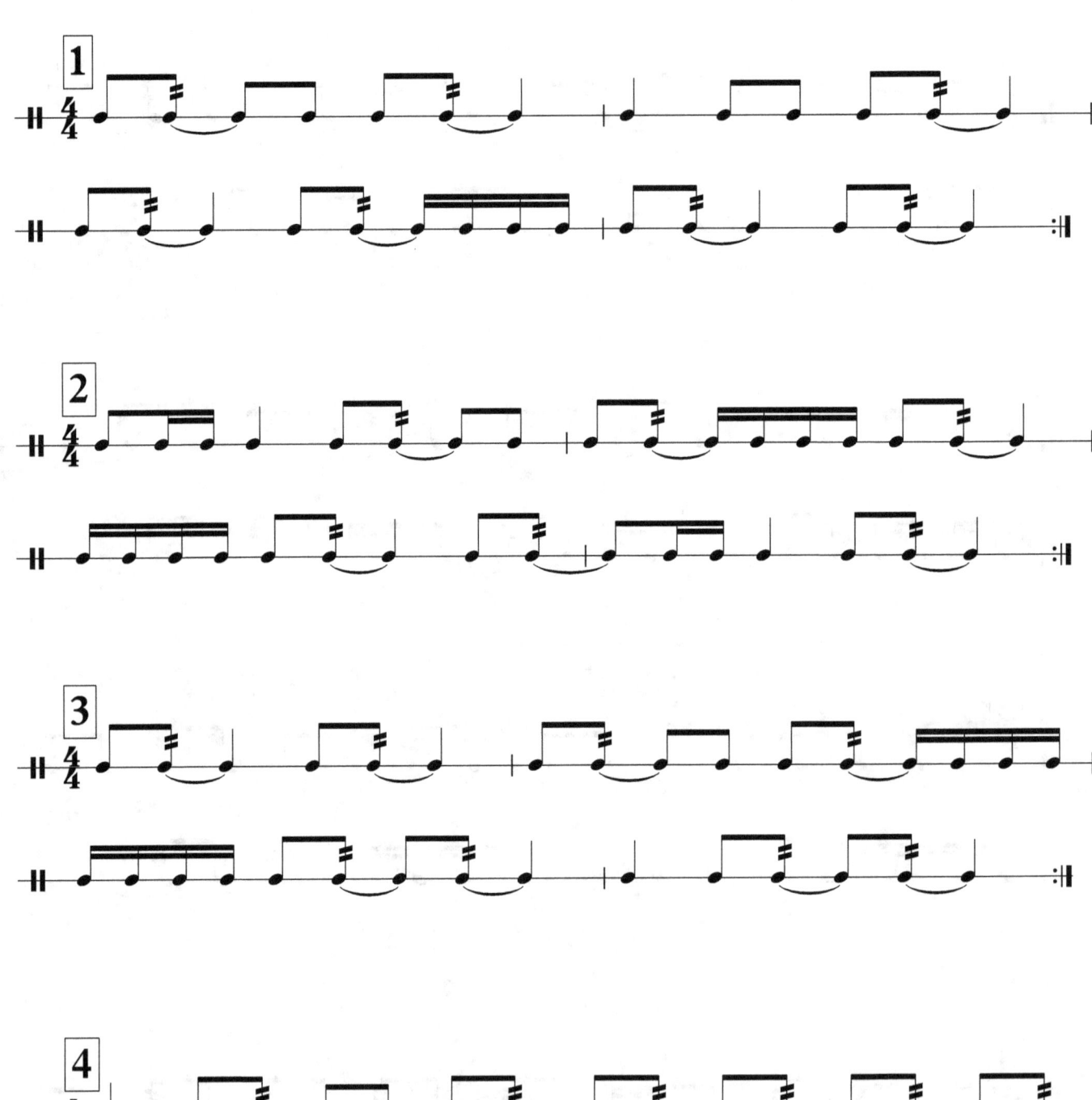

Lesson 8.8

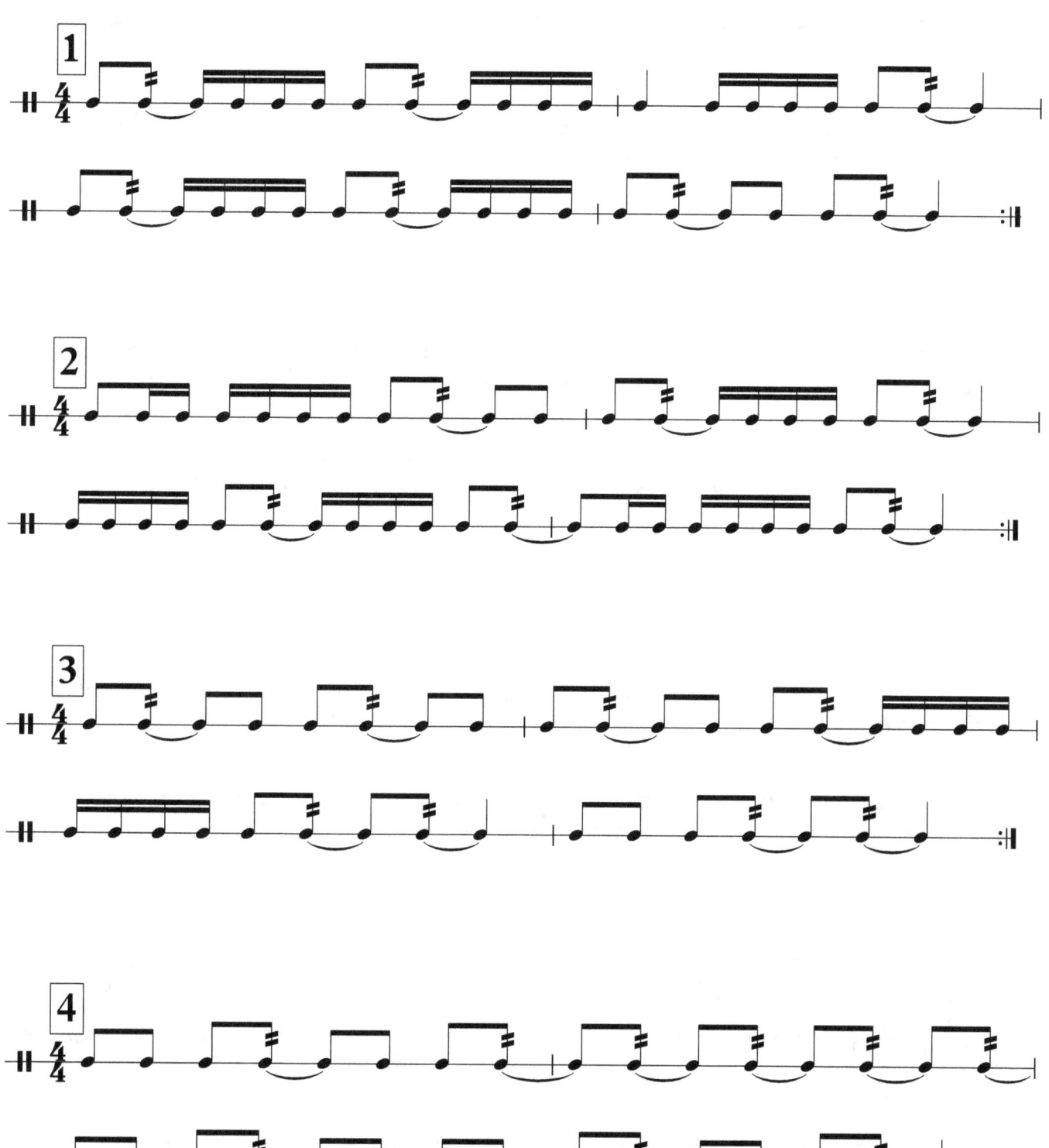

Lesson 8.9

Rhythm Review

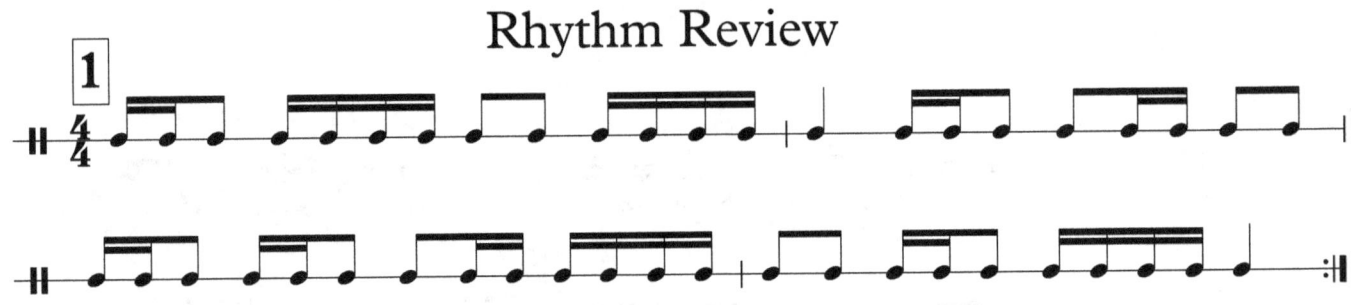

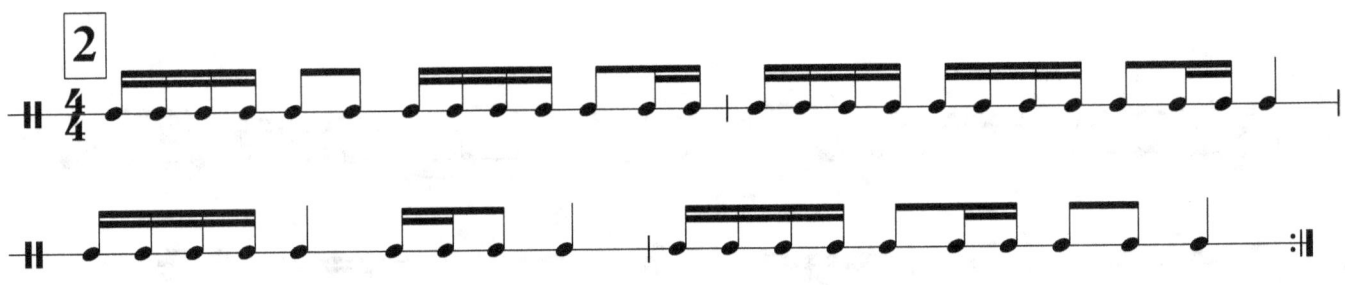

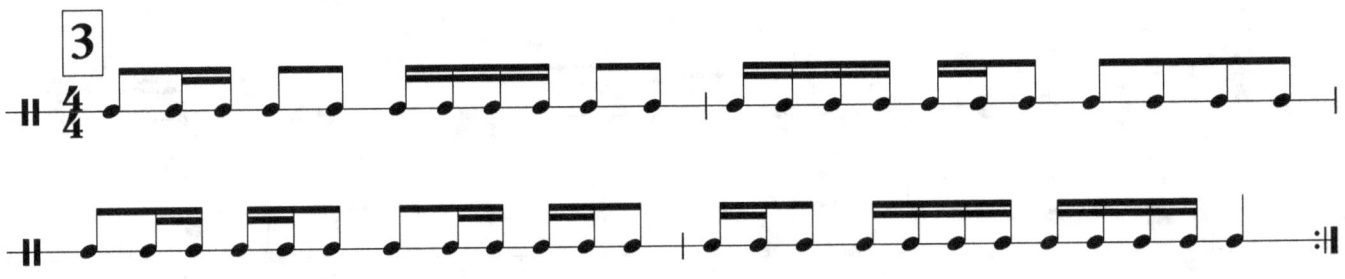

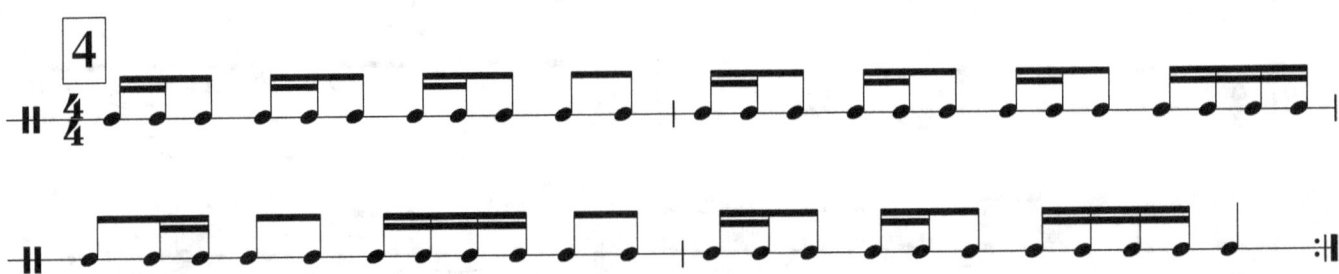

Unit 9

The Half Note Rest
The Whole Note Rest

A single Half note looks like this:　♩　　The Half note will receive two beat of sound.

A single Half rest looks like this:　▬　　The Half rest will receive two beats of silence.

A Whole Note looks like this:　**O**　　The Whole Note will receive four beats of sound.

The Whole Rest looks like this:　▬　　The Whole Rest will receive four beats of silence.

As a snare drummer, when you encounter a half note or whole note, it will usually be as a roll. You will occasionally see these notes written for rebound strokes. If so, you simply strike the drum on the first beat of the note and count the rest of the note as if you are resting. This unit, will provide practice on half and whole notes as rolls.

The Half Note roll looks like this:　　　　The Half Note roll is played like this:

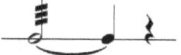
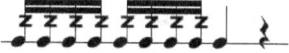

The Whole Note roll looks like this:　　　The Whole Note roll is played like this:

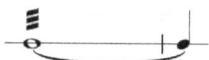
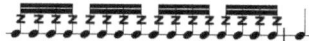

All rolls should be thought of as rhythms. It is very important that you are counting carefully when playing a long roll. Hand motion will be key to the correct timing of the release.

Lesson 9.1

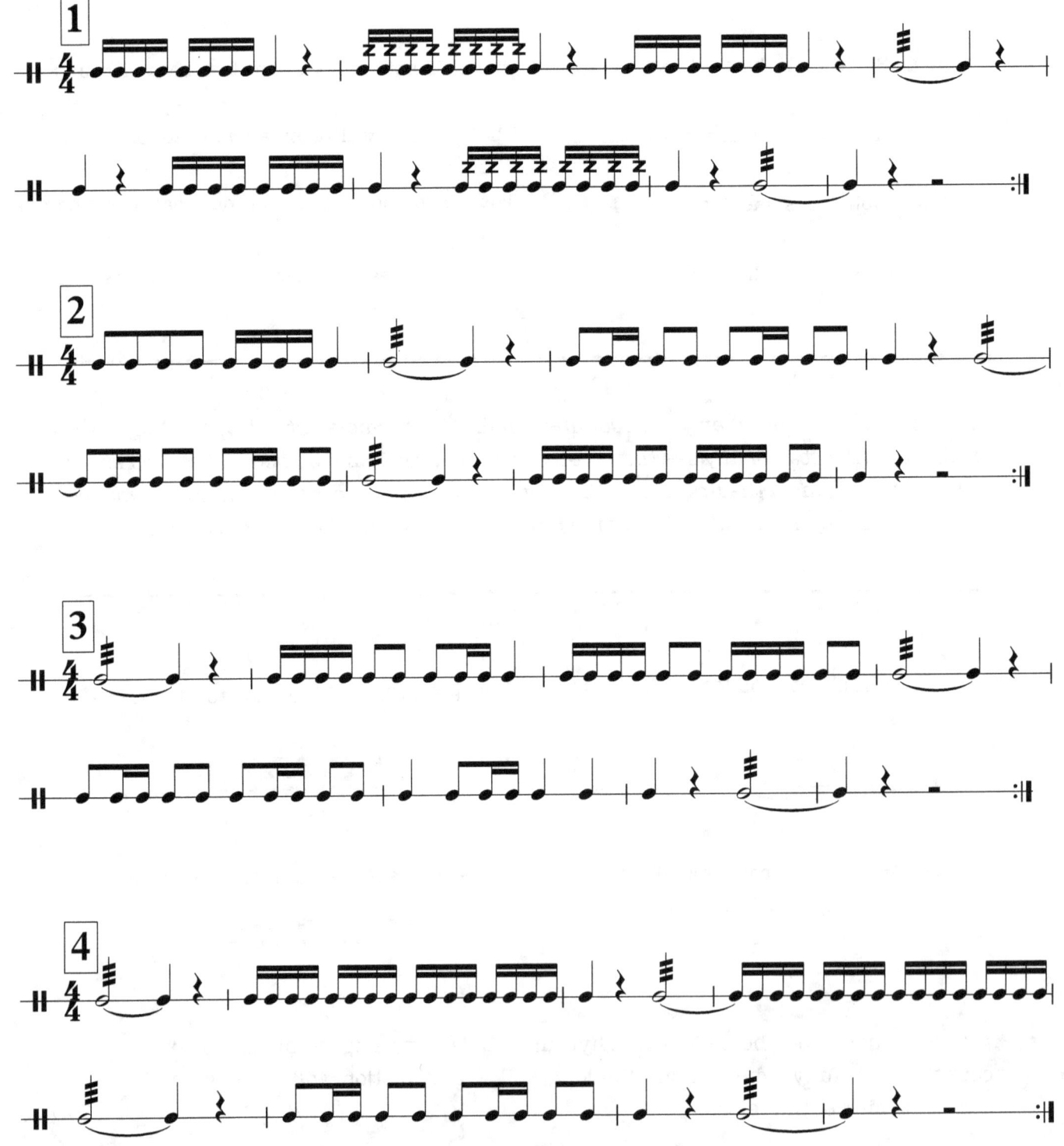

Lesson 9.2

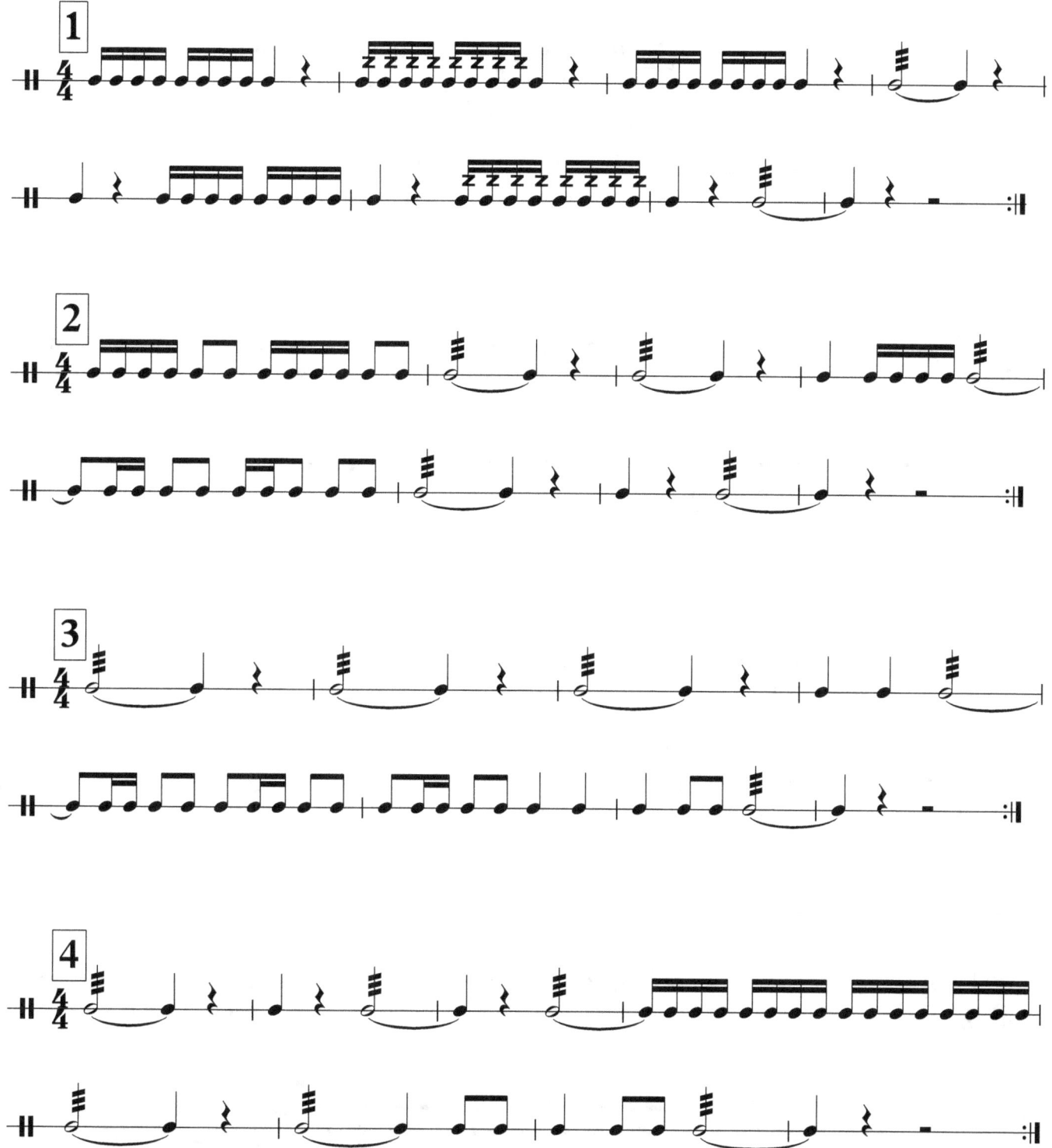

Lesson 9.3

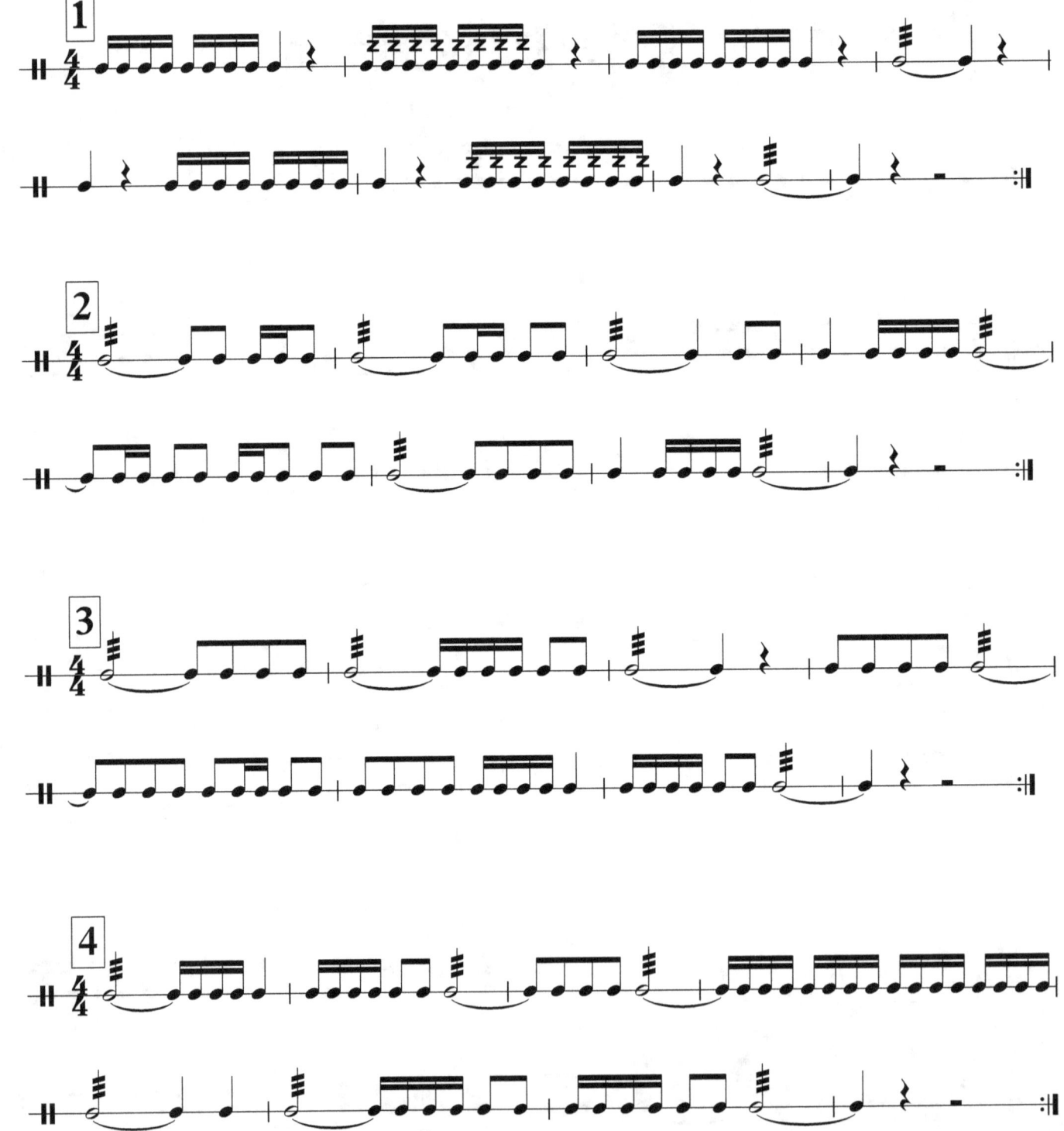

Lesson 9.4

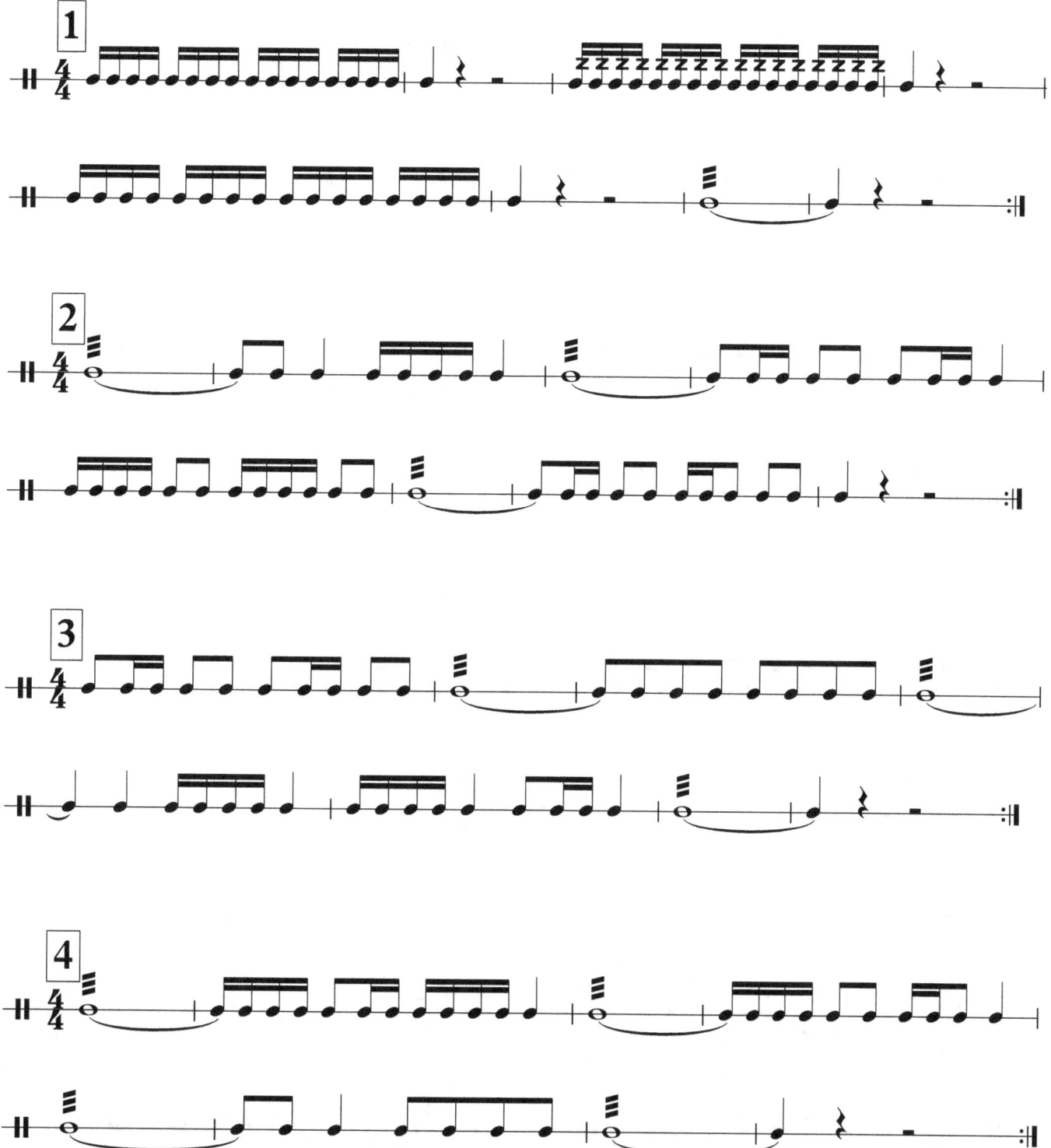

Lesson 9.5

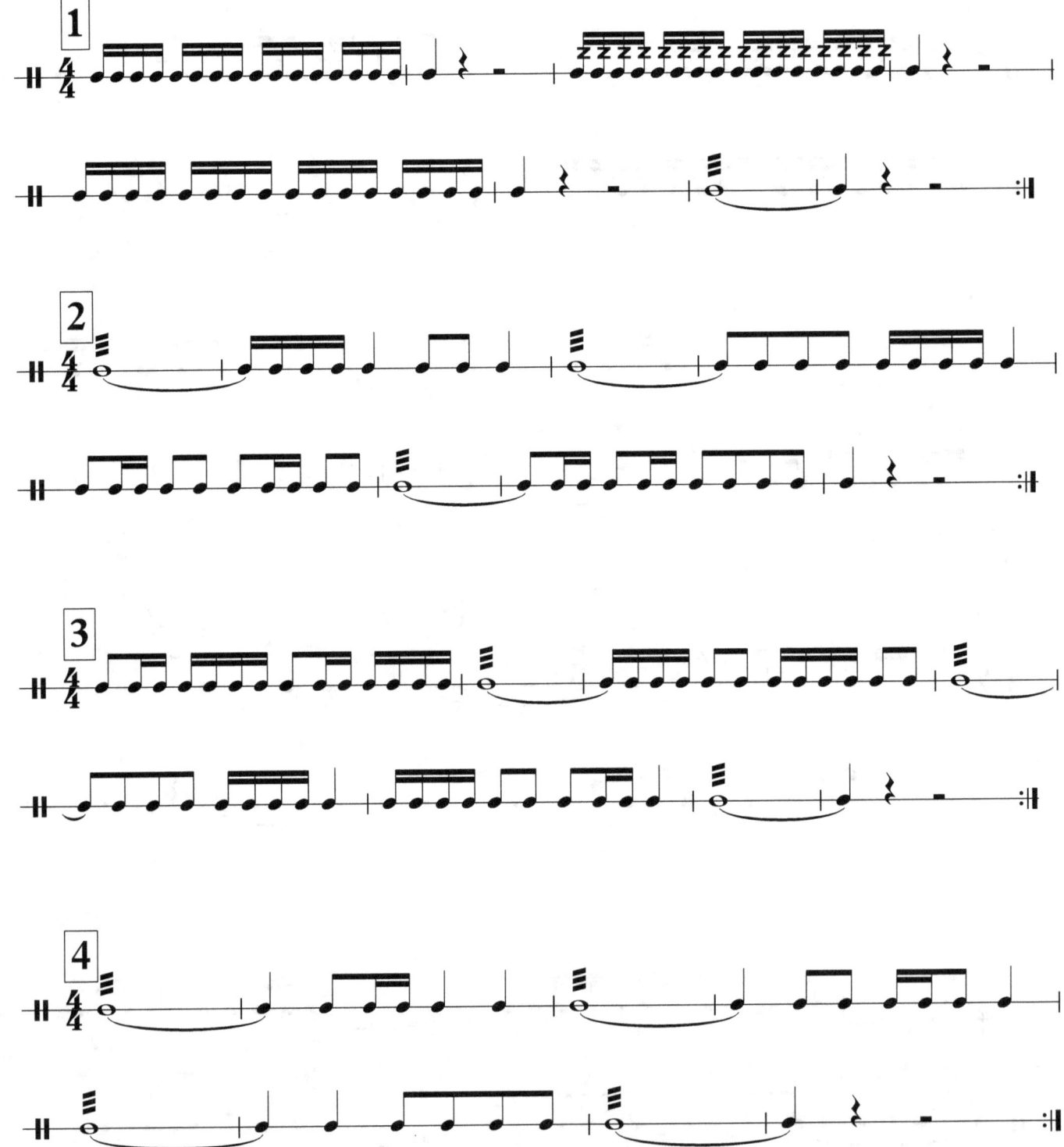

Lesson 9.6

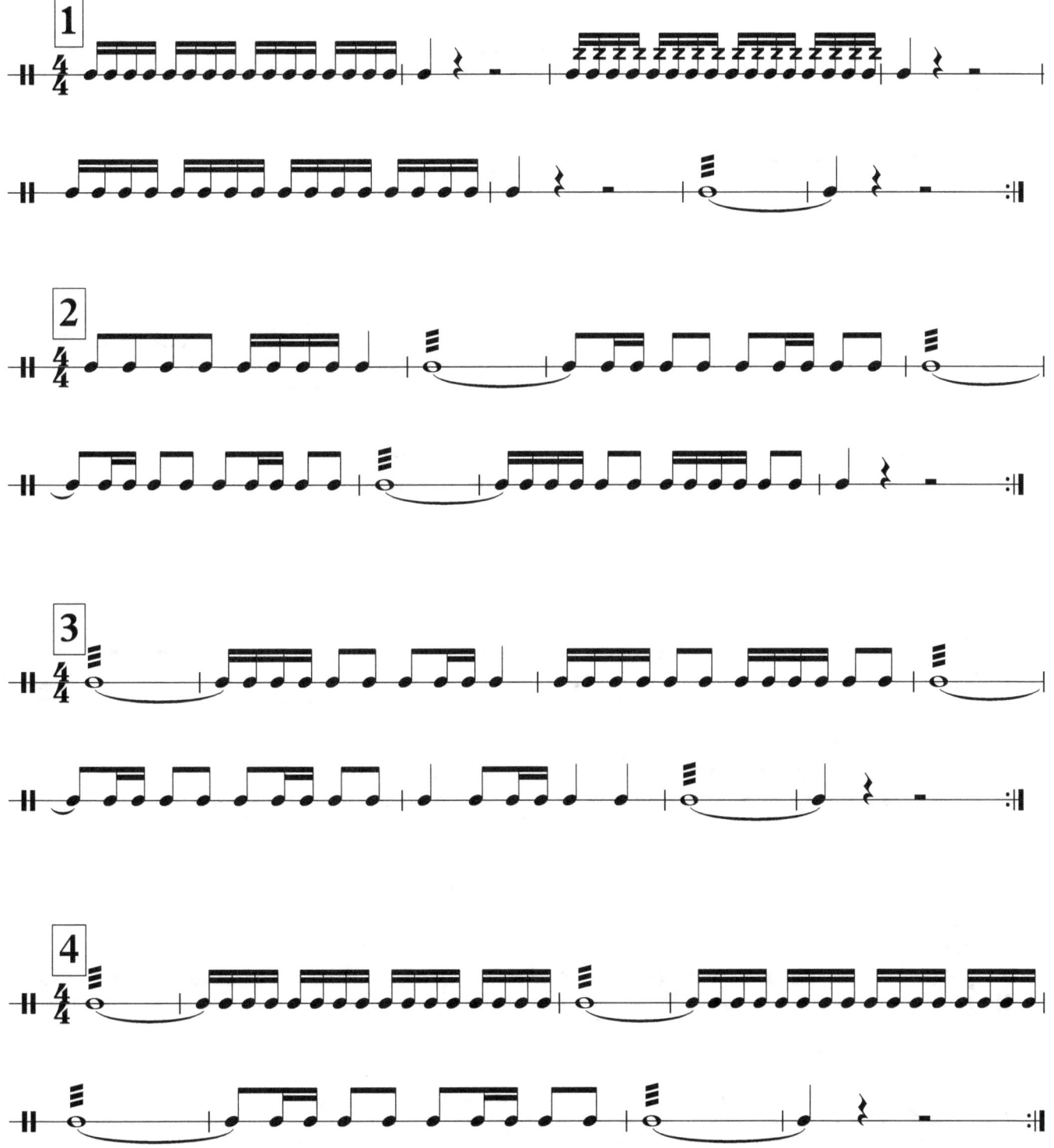

73

Lesson 9.7

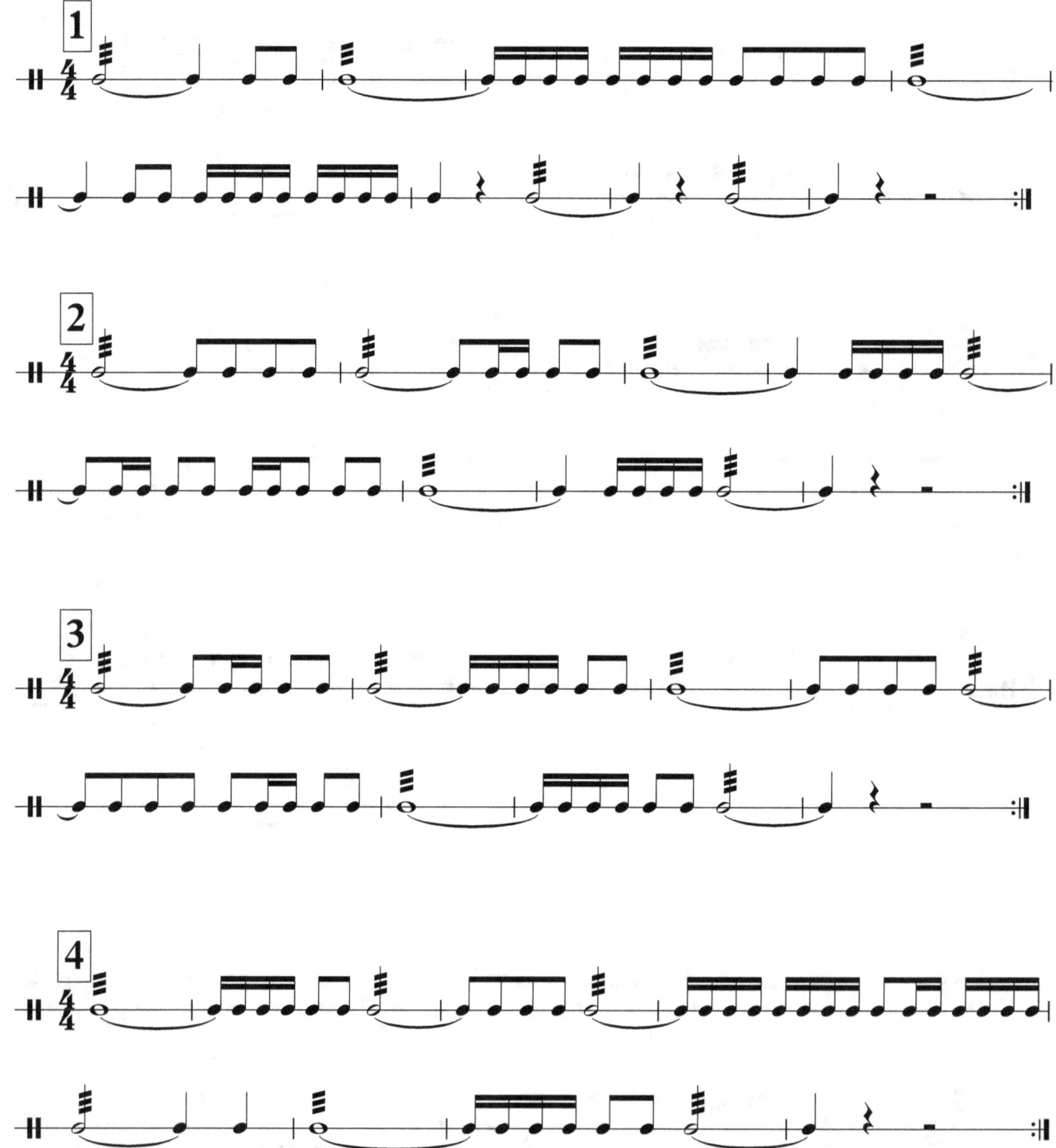

Unit 10

The Eighth Rest

An Eighth Rest looks like this:

An Eighth Rest takes up 1/2 of a beat.

An Eighth Rest is counted like an eighth note.

Two eighth notes in a row are sticked "R-L". When an eighth rest is on the beat, eliminate the R hand Stroke. The stickings will be written in for the first page of exercises to solidify the concept.

Lesson 10.1

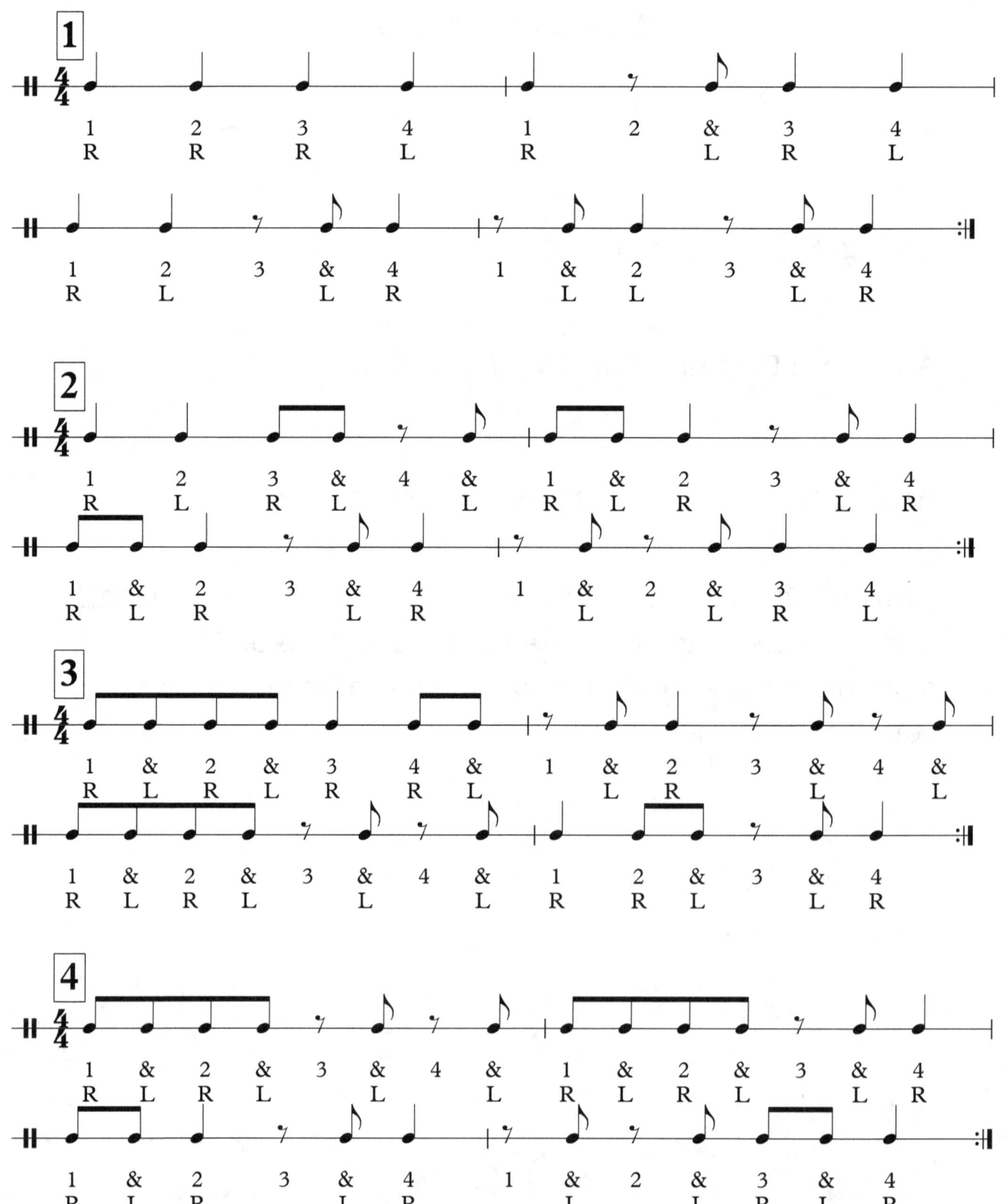

Lesson 10.2

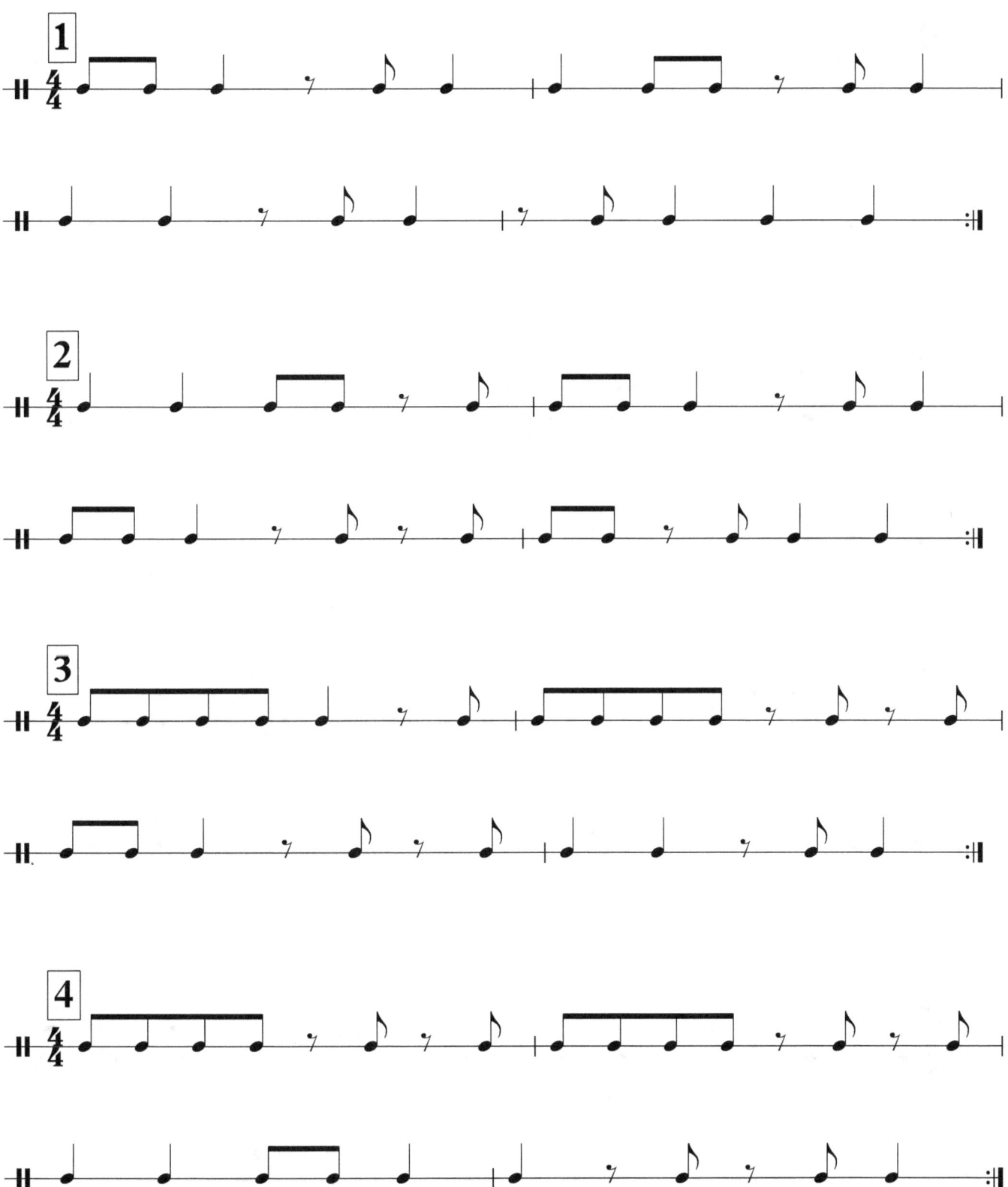

Lesson 10.3

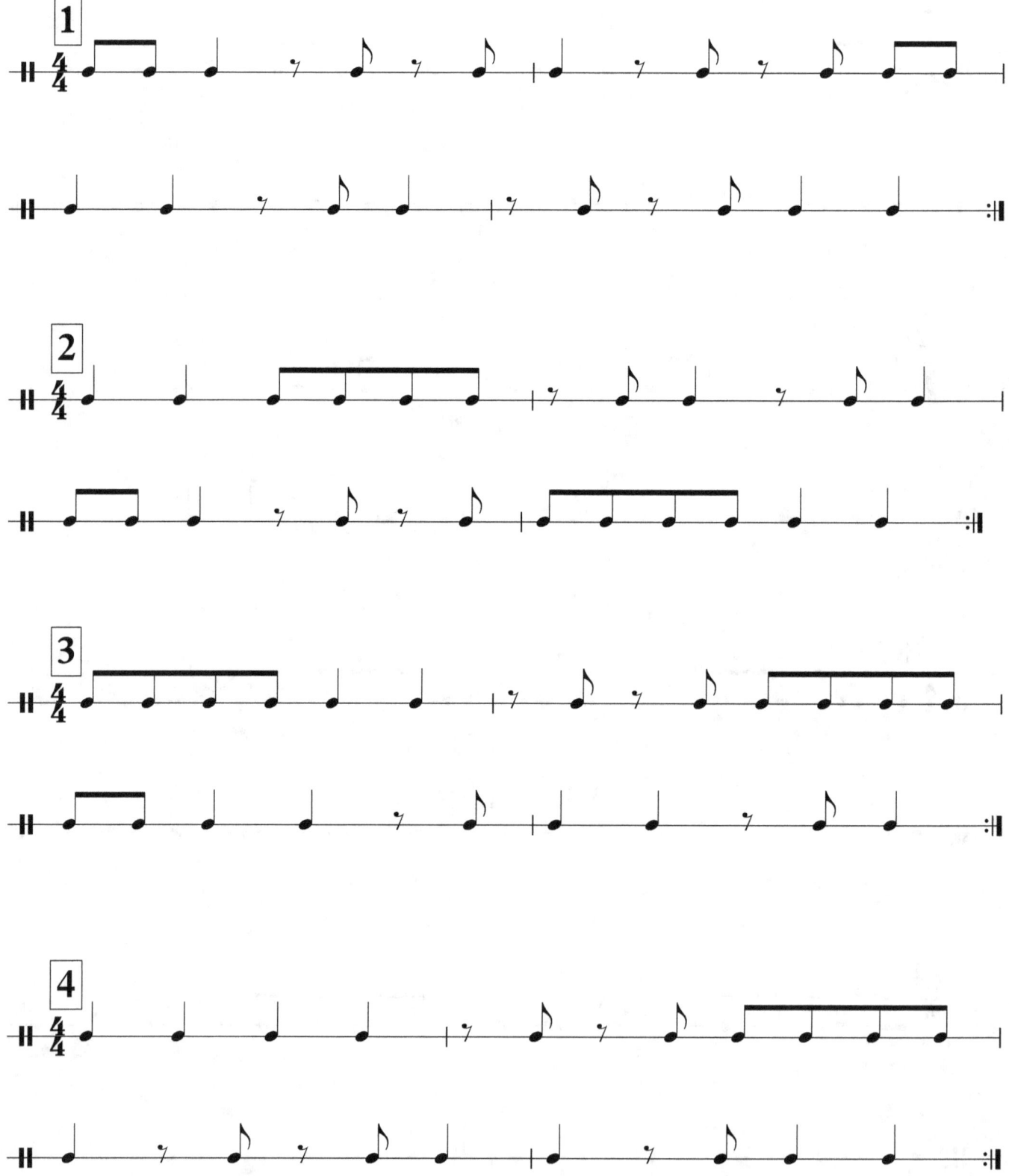

Lesson 10.4

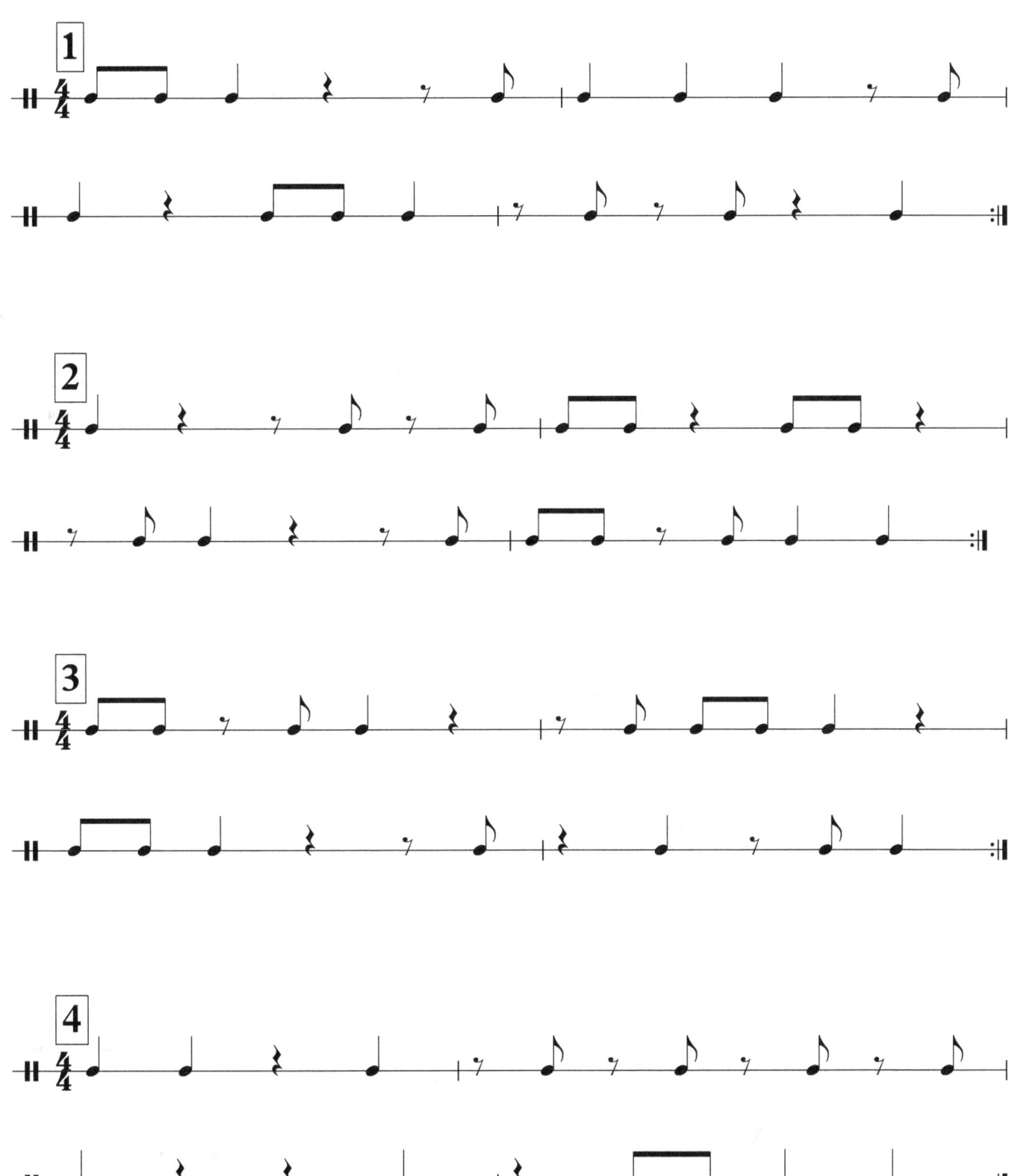

Lesson 10.5

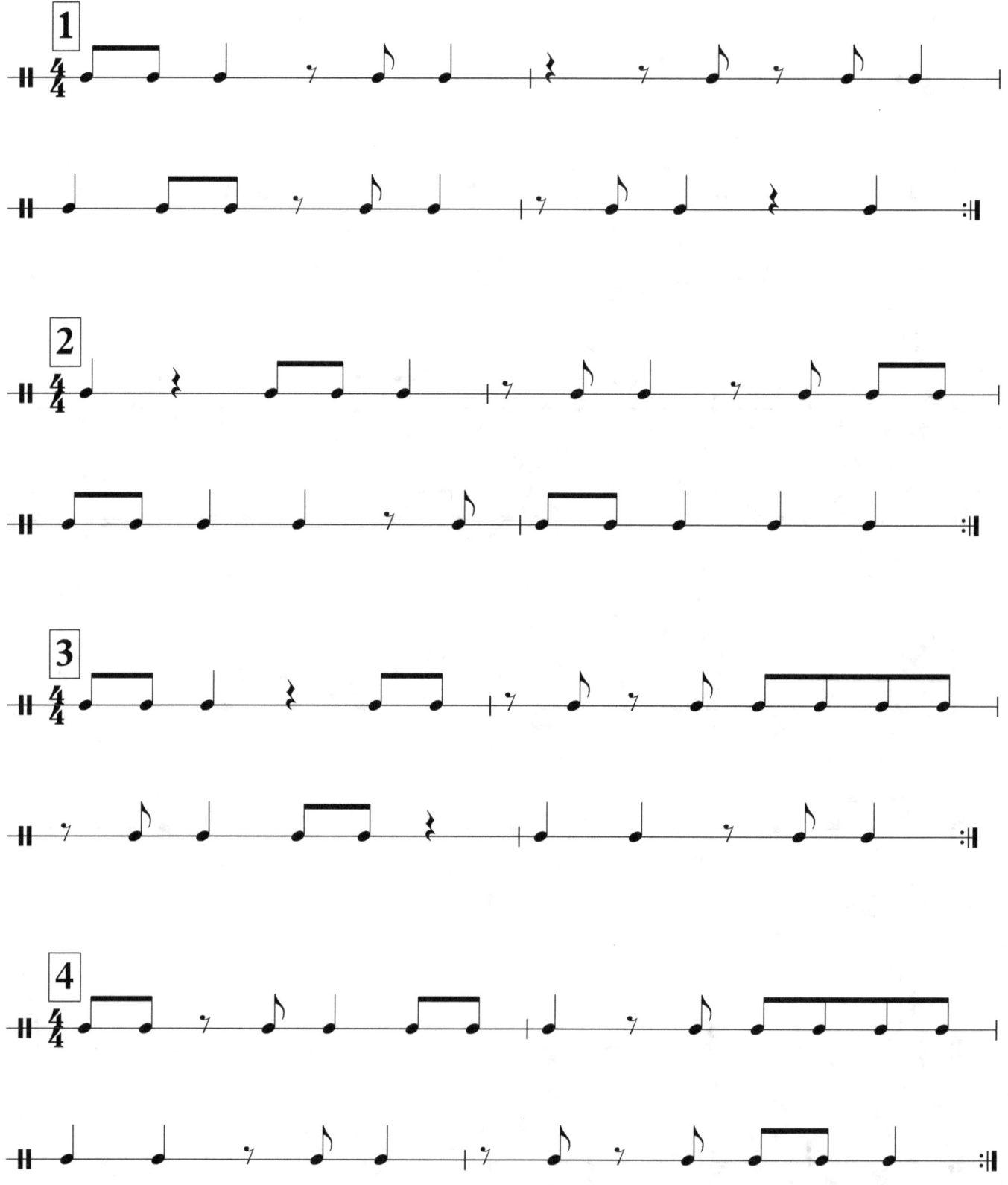

Lesson 10.6

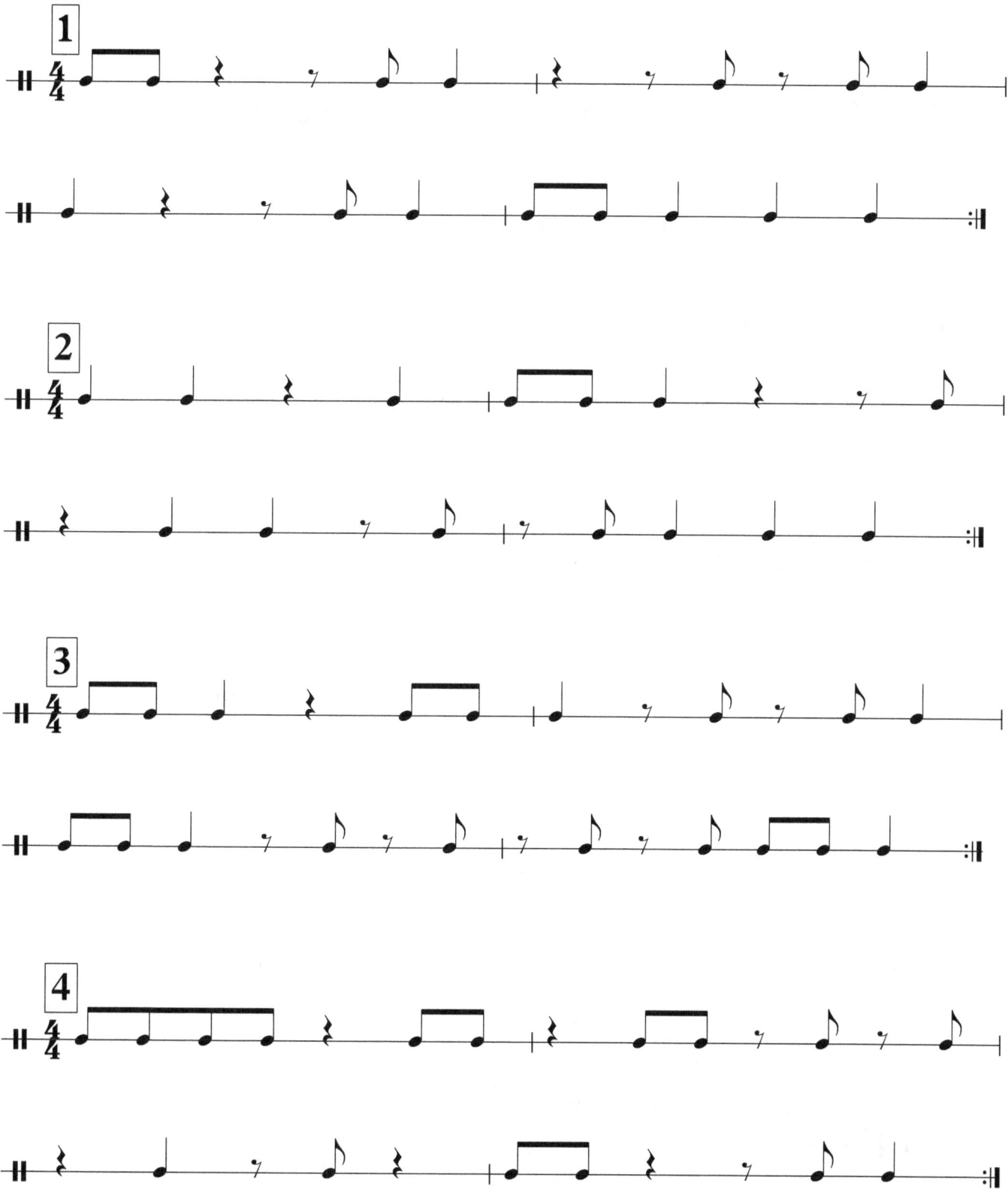

Unit 11

The Downstroke, Tap, Upstroke and Accents

The **Downstroke** is used to stop the stick from rebounding too high off of the drum head. To perform a Downstroke, strike the drum and just after impact, squeeze the stick SLIGHTLY with the fulcrum and back fingers. A good goal is to try and stop the stick 2 inches off of the drum head.

The **TAP** is a soft, relaxed wrist stroke played 2-3 inches above the drum.

Practice each exercise RH alone and then LH alone.

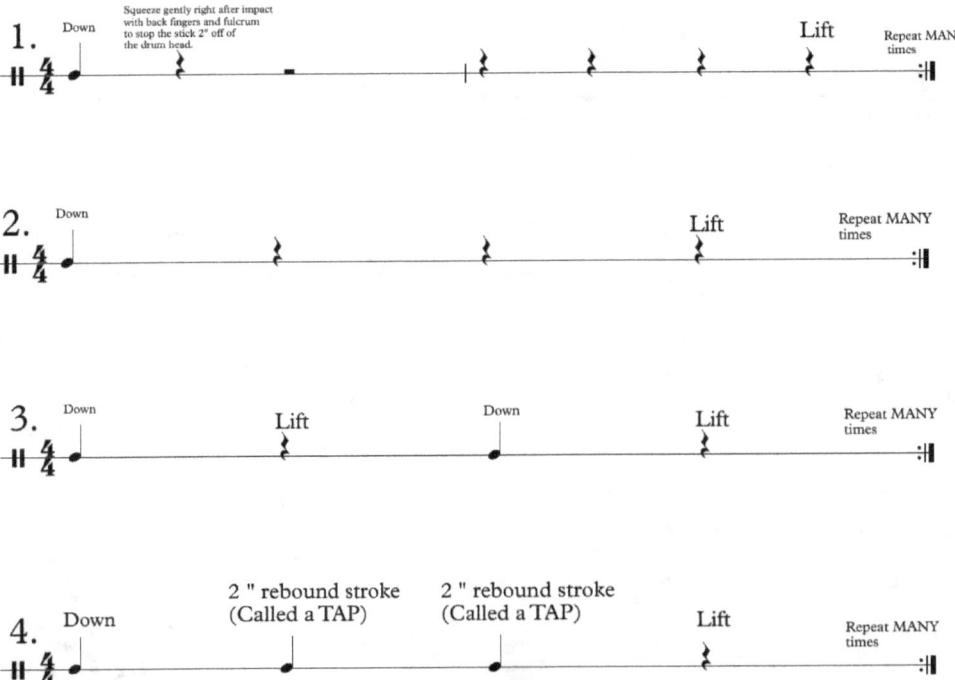

The **Upstroke** is used to set up the downstroke. After the tap stroke is performed, lift the stick to the desired height. Practice the following exercises RH alone and LH alone.

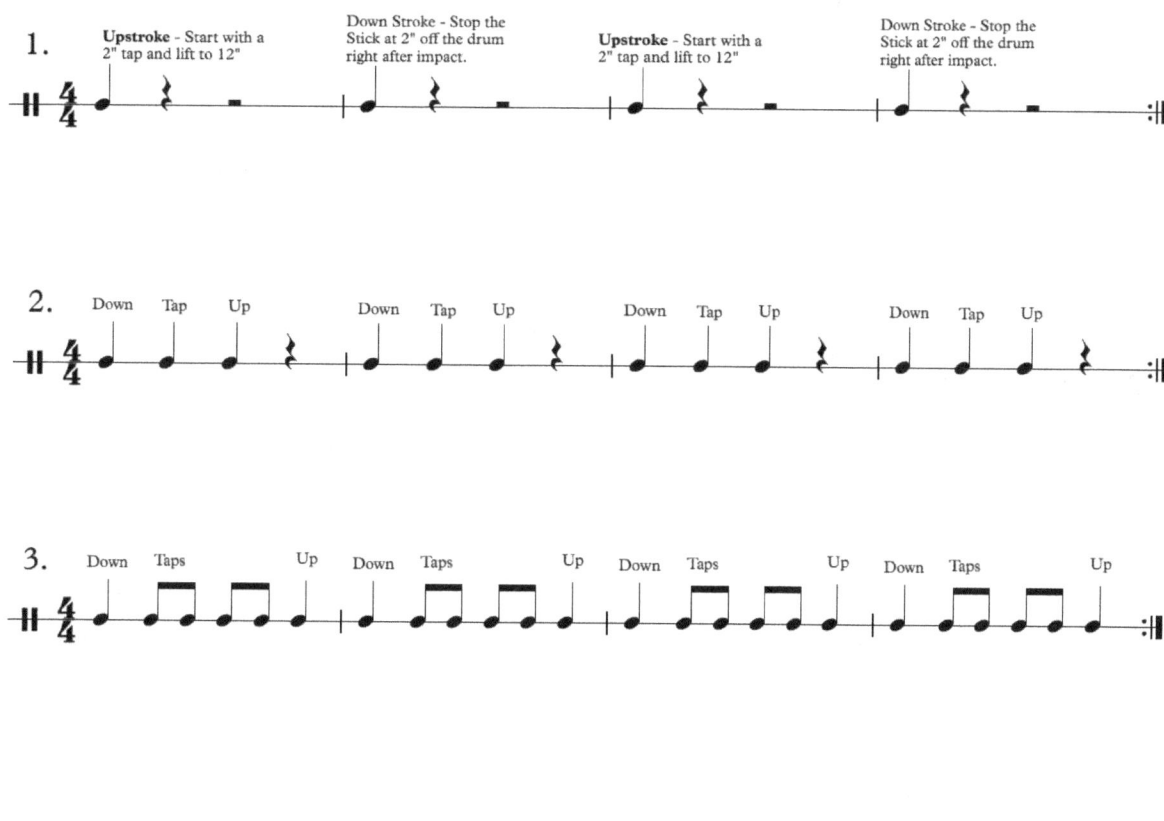

*** This symbol (>) that is in in exercise 4 is called an **accent**. It means to emphasis that note. When playing an accent on the snare drum, lift the stick a little higher for that note. Often times an accent is played as a downstroke, unless it is followed by another accent.

The exercises on the following page are all based off of rhythms from earlier exercises. In this unit, accents have been added. Play all non-accented notes at 3" and play the accented notes at 9". You will need to use Downstrokes, Upstrokes, Rebound Strokes and Taps.

Lesson 11.1

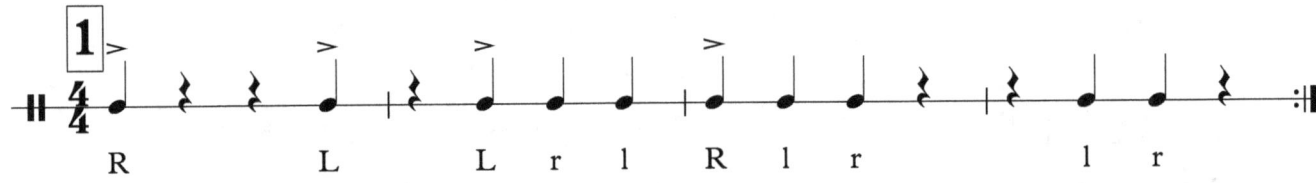

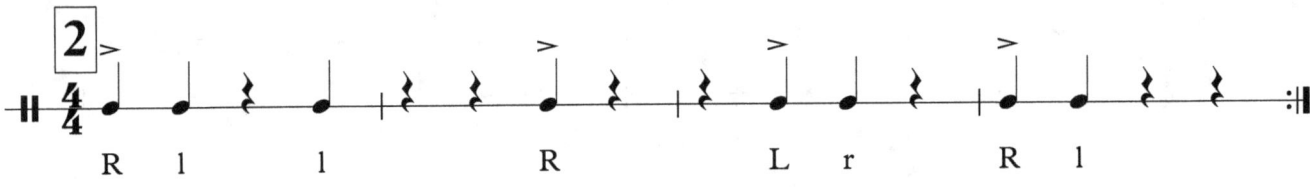

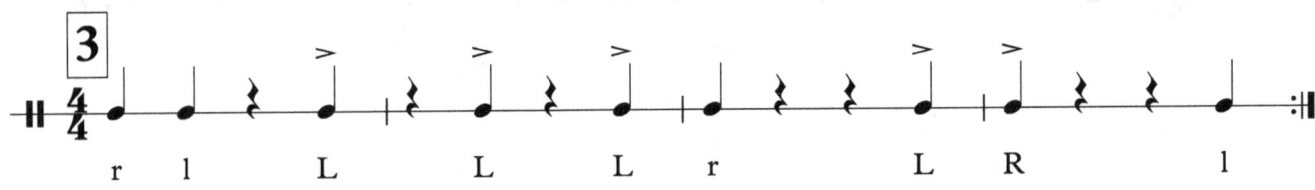

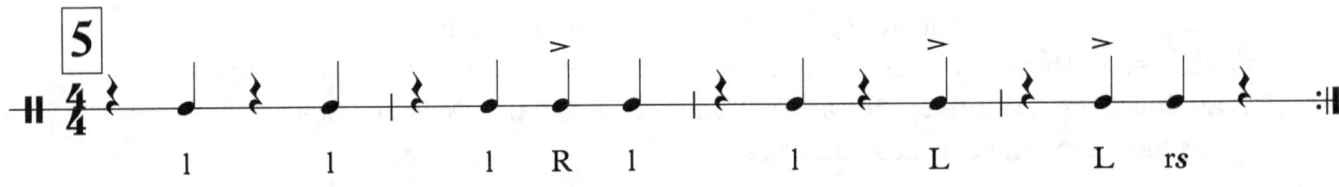

Lesson 11.2

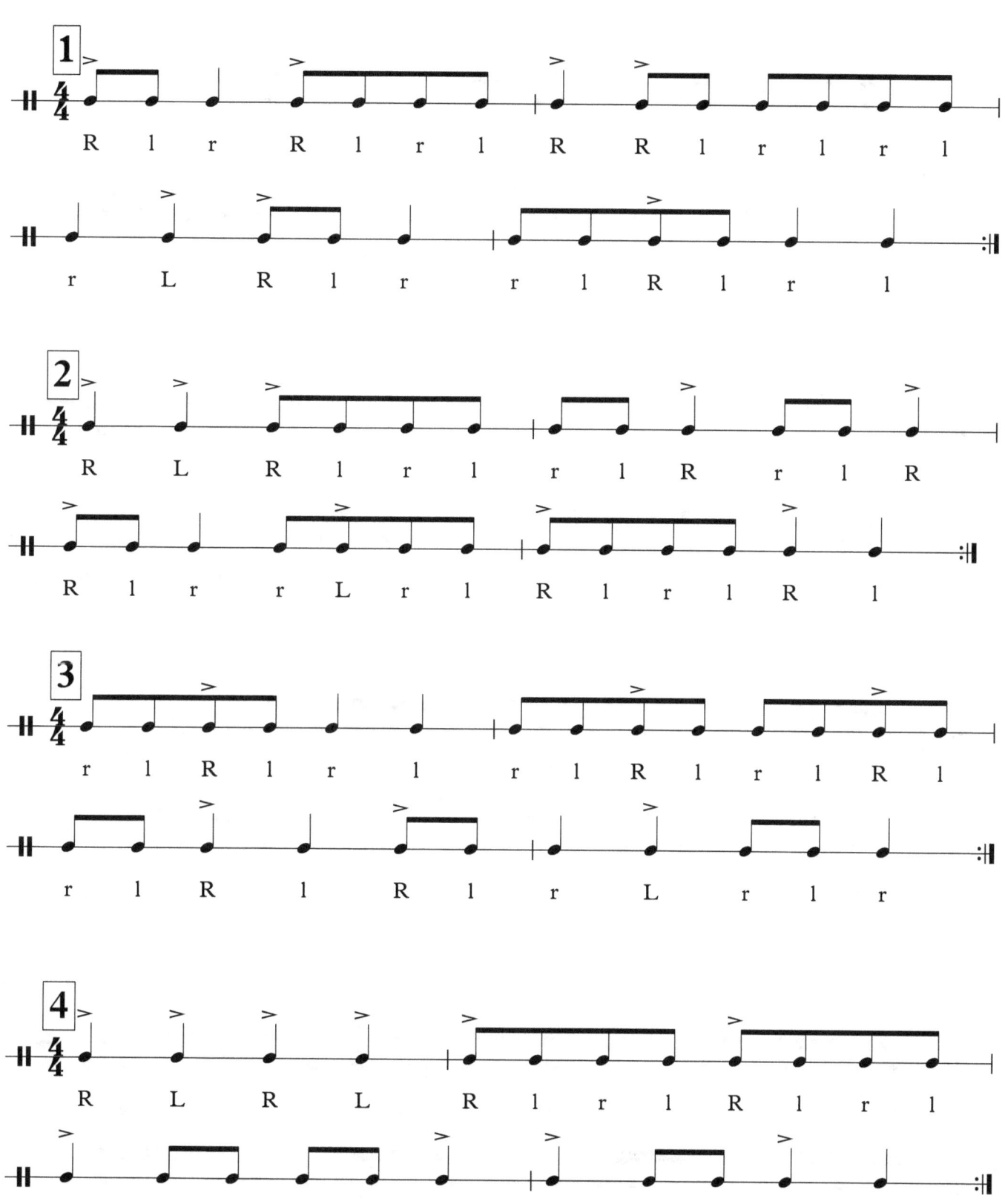

Lesson 11.3

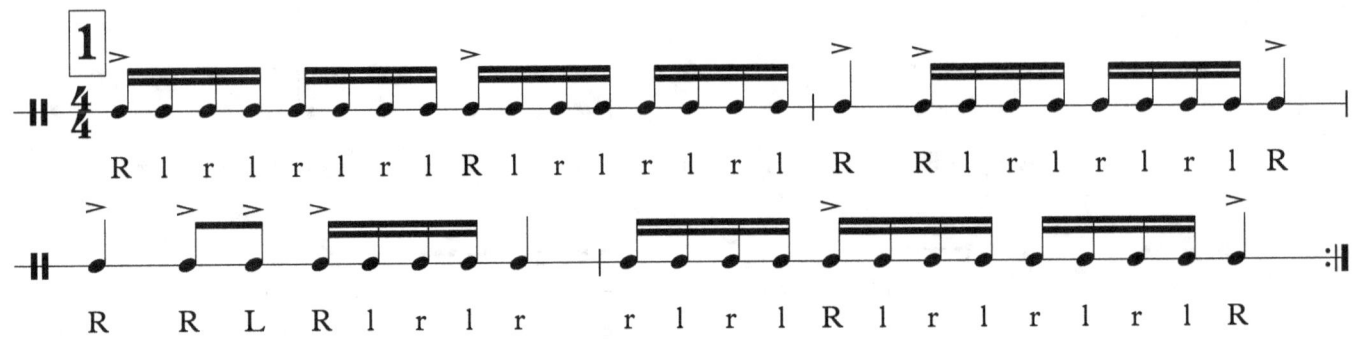

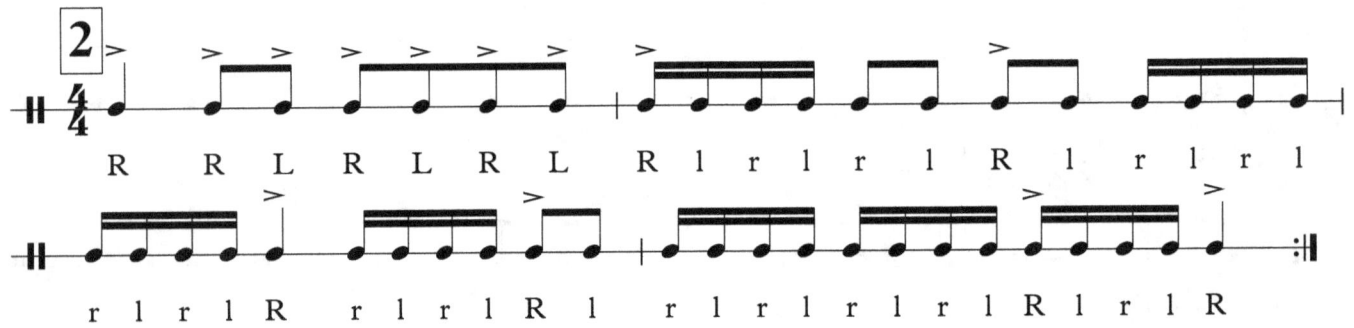

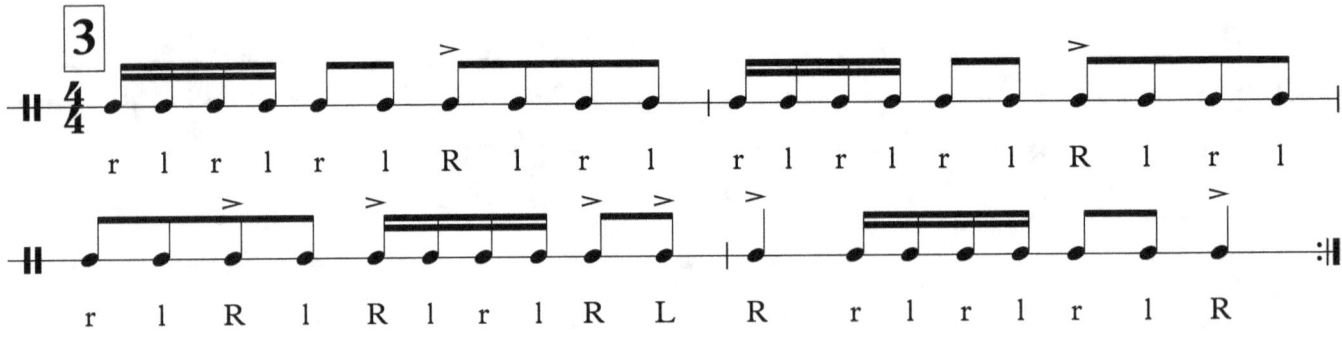

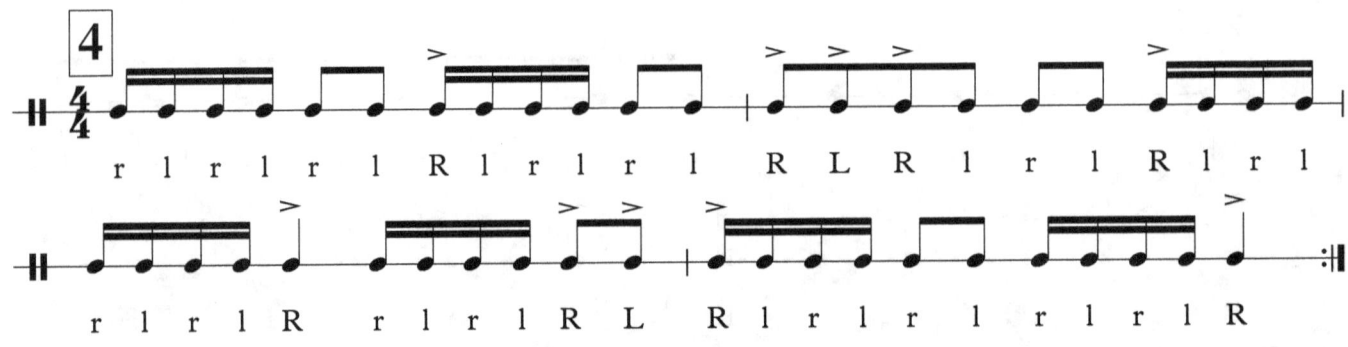

Lesson 11.4

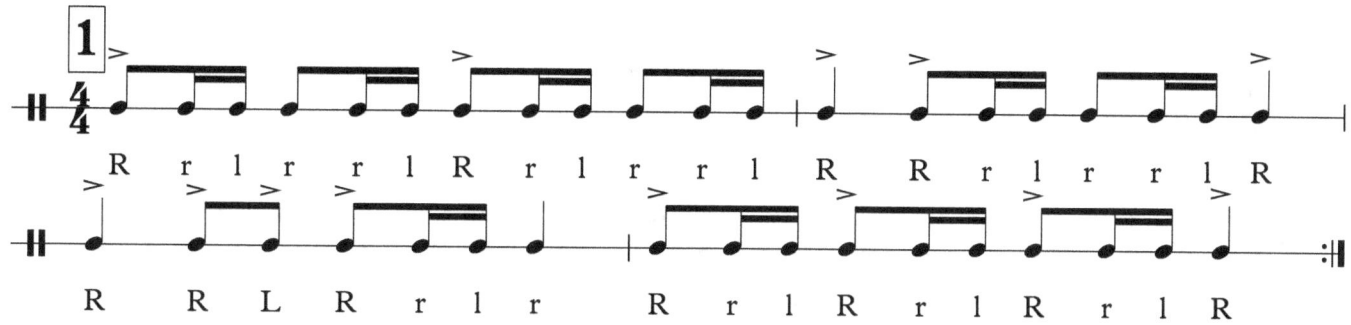

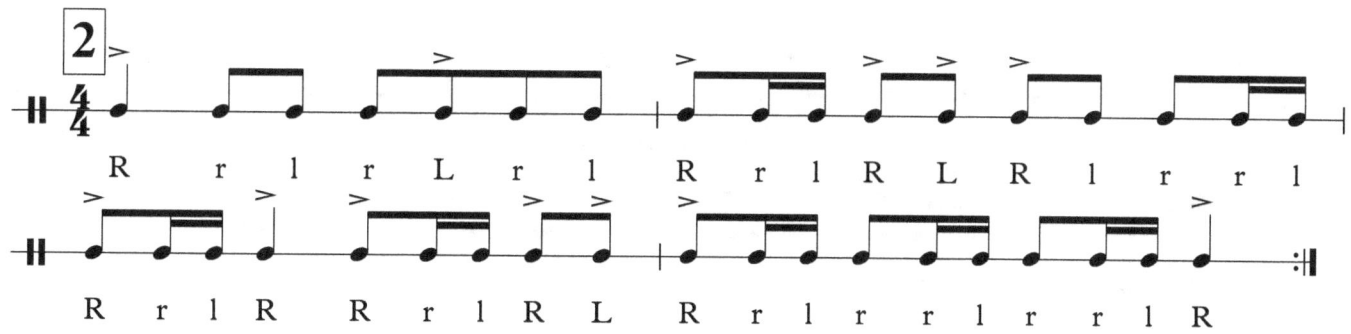

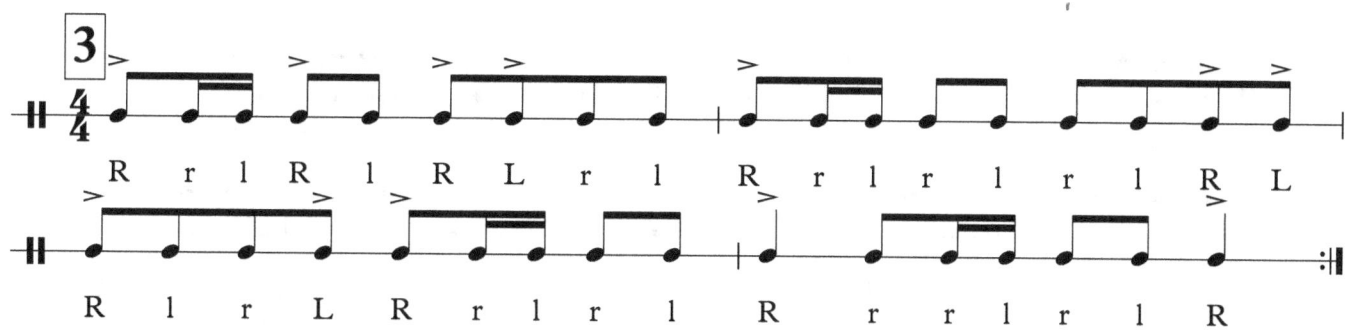

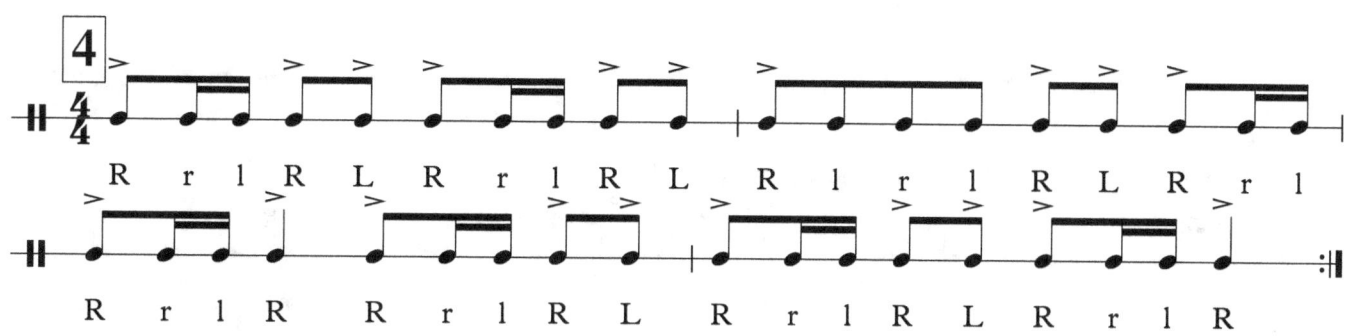

Lesson 11.5

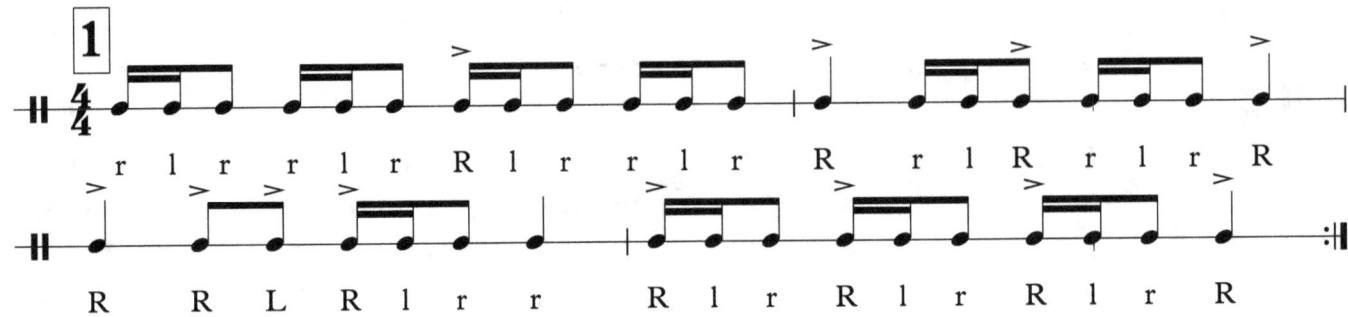

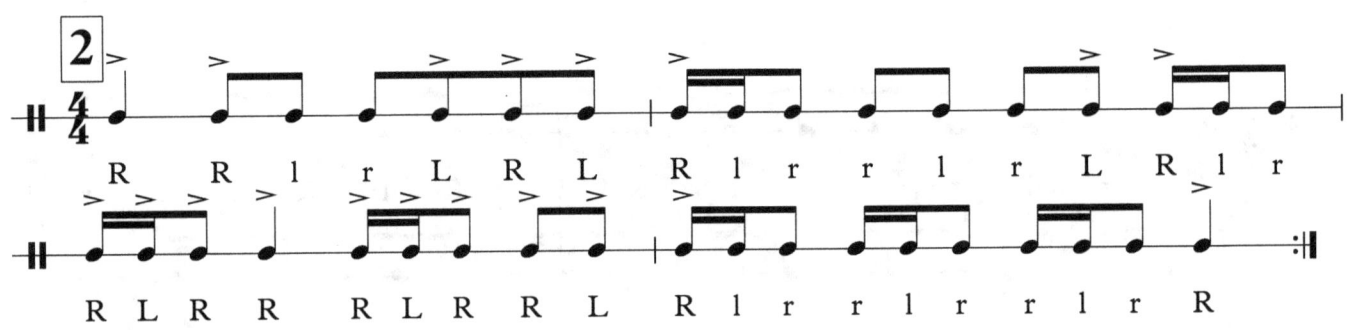

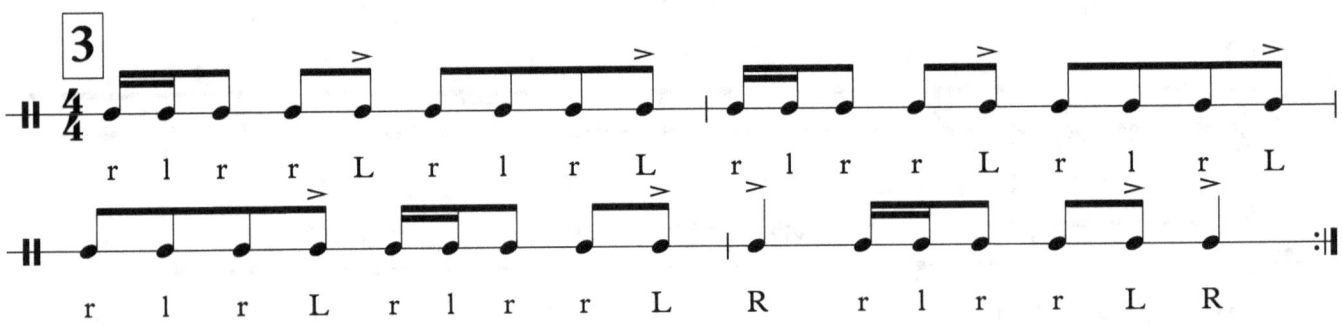

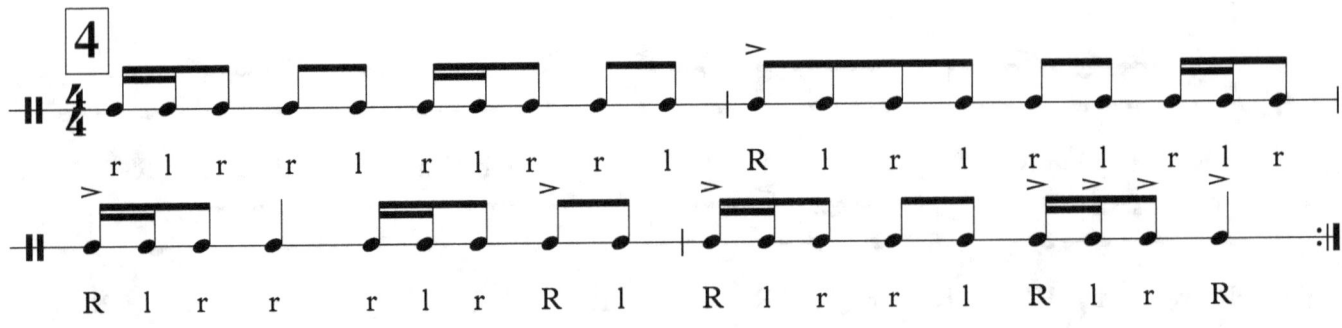

Lesson 11.6

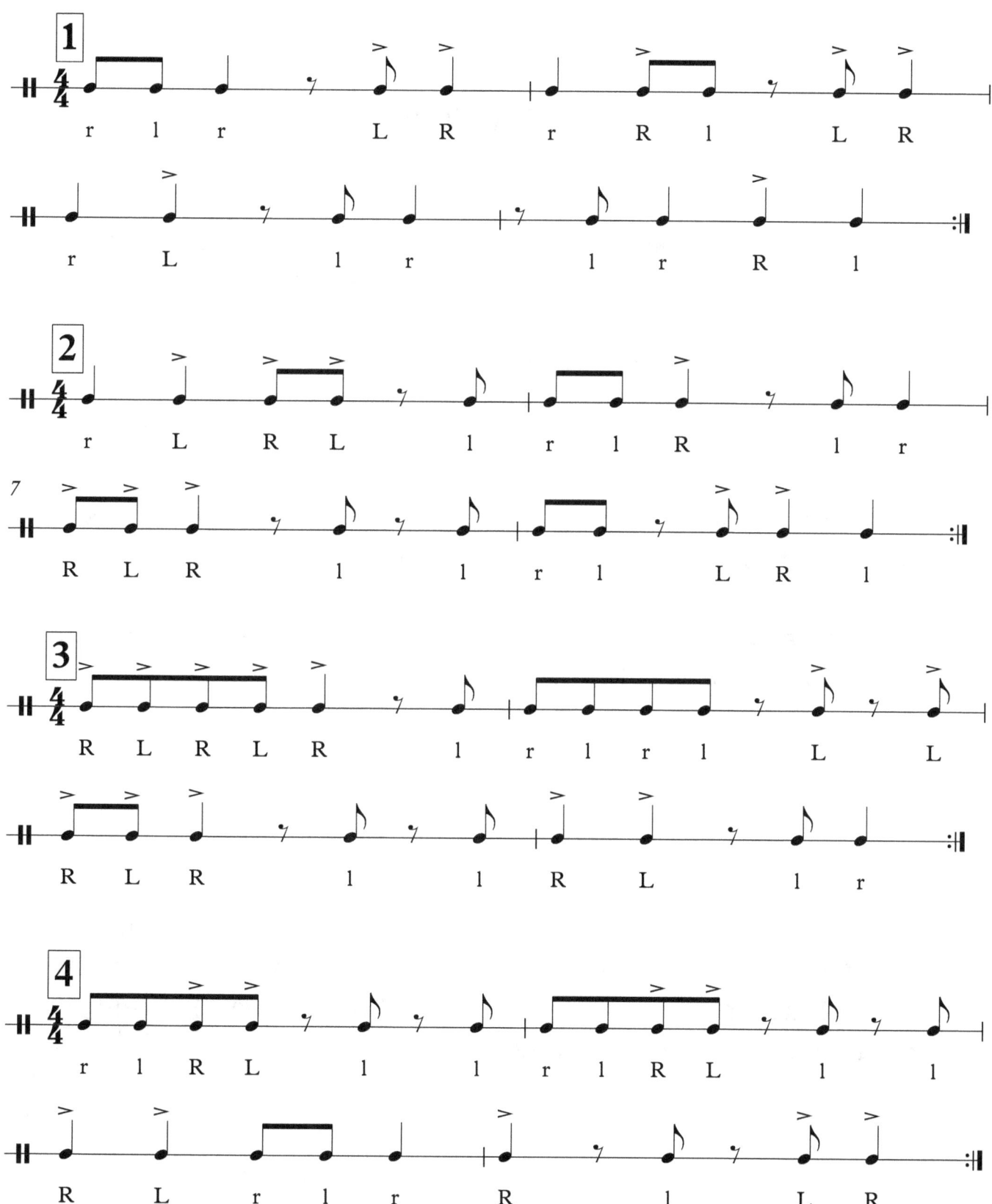

Unit 12

The Flam

The Flam is a combination of two strokes to make one sound. The two strokes are the **Primary stroke** and a **Grace note**.

The Primary stroke should be played as a normal rebound or downstroke (depending on what follows). It will look like a normal note.

The Grace note should be played no higher than 2". It will look like a "tiny" note that comes just before the Primary Stroke.

Here is what a RH Flam looks like, followed by a LH Flam. The Flam name corresponds with the hand of the Primary Stroke.

The Grace note will hit just before the Primary stroke. The Flam should sound like "chet" when played correctly. Try to avoid the two strokes hitting at the same time (This is called a flat flam) or being too far apart (this is called a wide flam)

There are many ways that the strokes of a Flam can be approached. It depends on what is following the flam. In this book, the goal is to play alternating Flams.

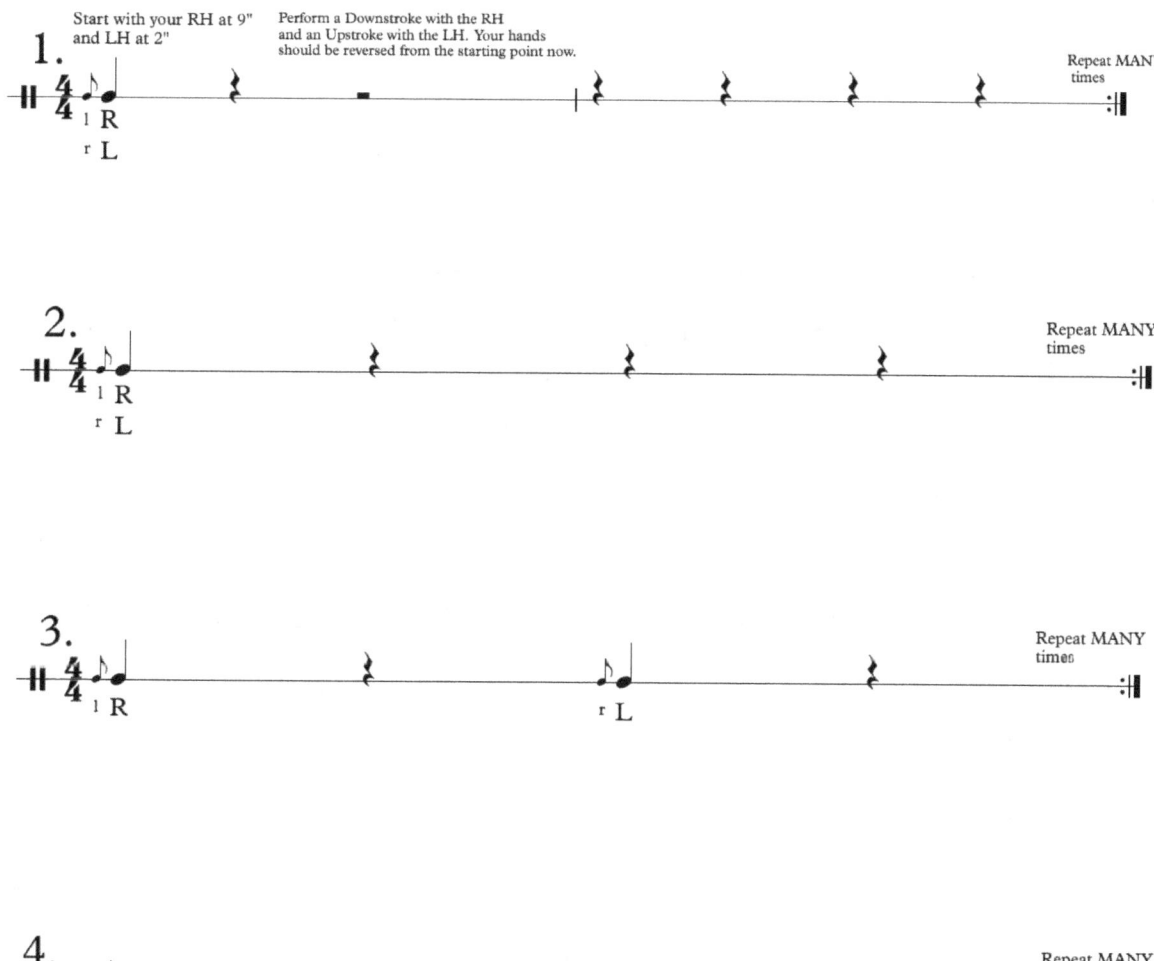

The exercises on the next page are all based off of rhythms from earlier exercises. In this unit, flams have been added. Play these exercises very slowly and think about what needs to happen to set up the flam and where the sticks should go after after the flam. Note – Only the primary stroke sticking is labeled. Assume the grace note will be played with the opposite hand.

Lesson 12.1

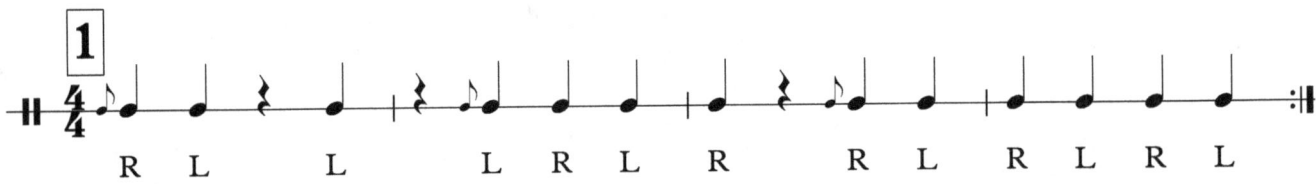

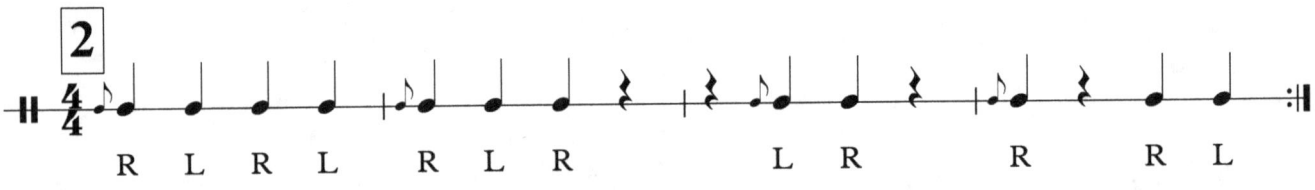

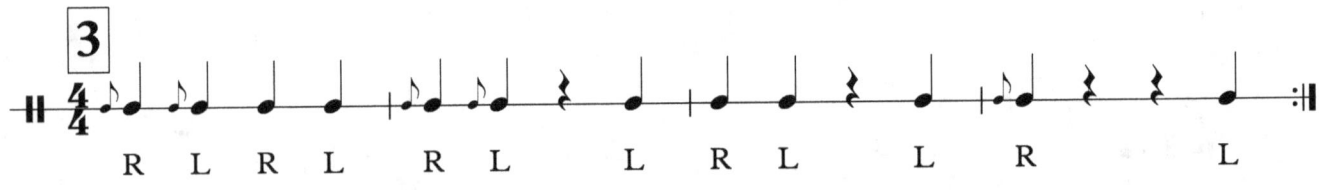

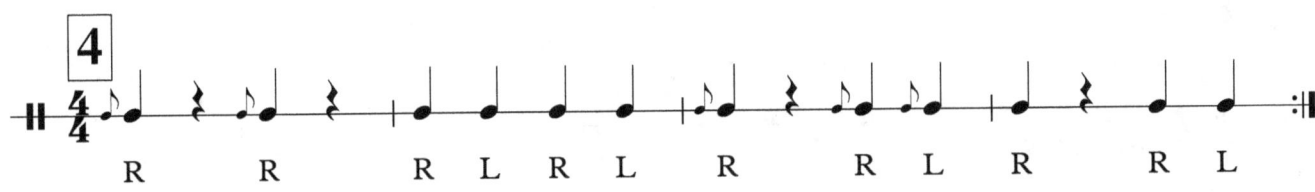

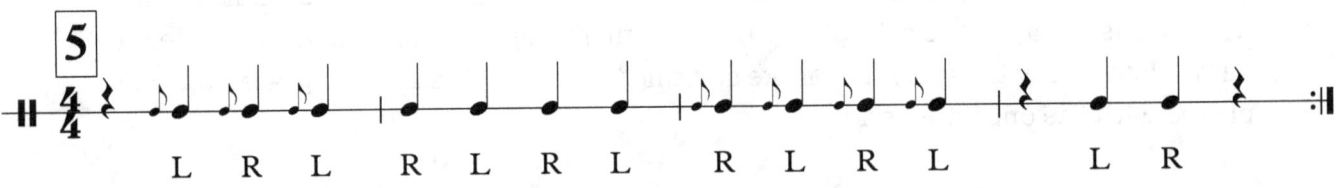

Lesson 12.2

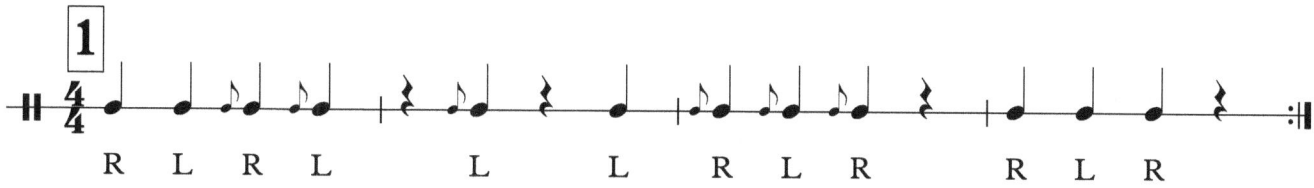

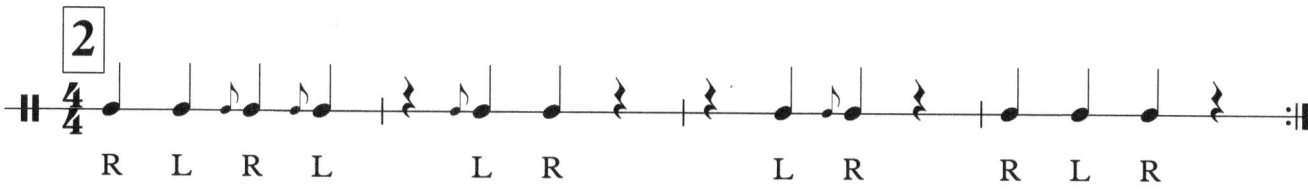

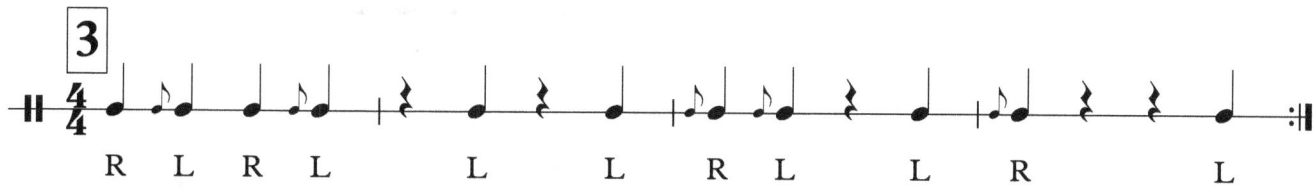

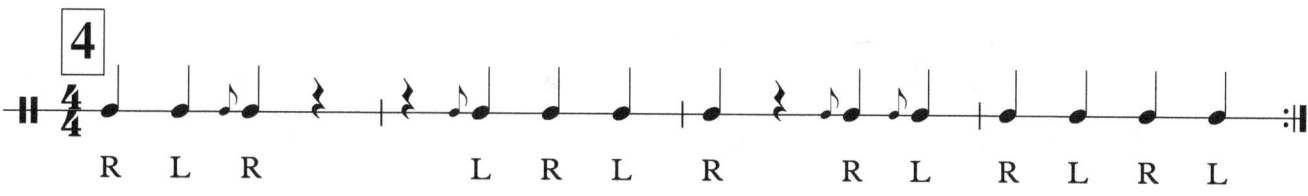

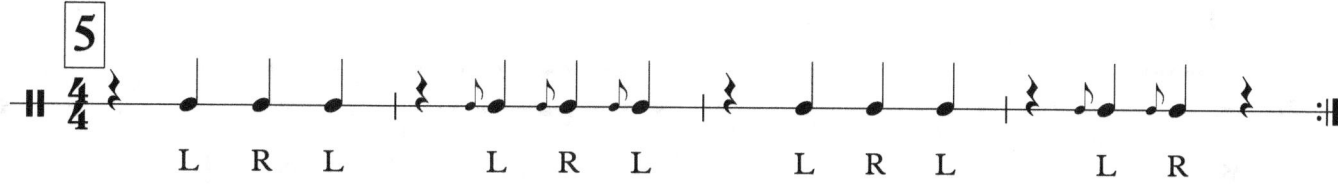

Lesson 12.3

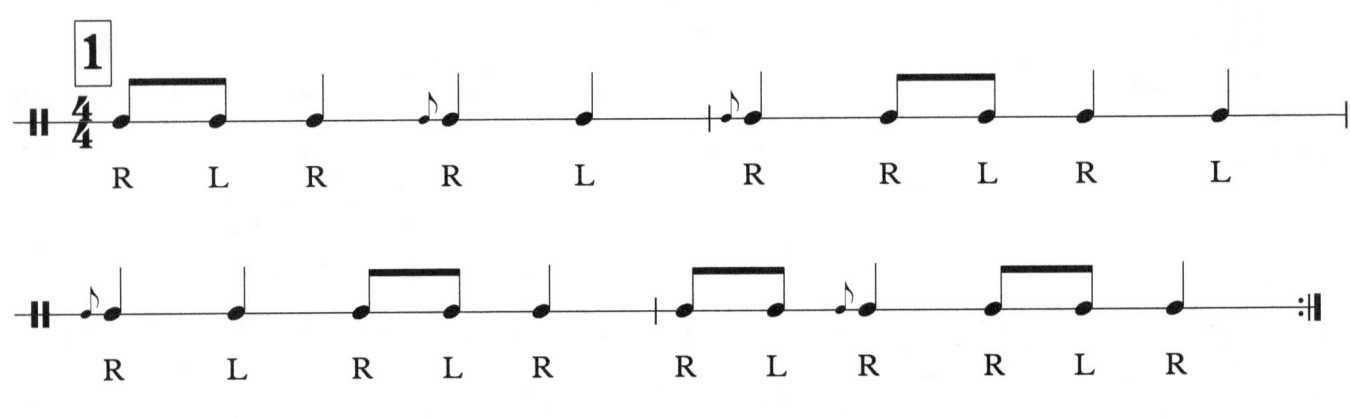

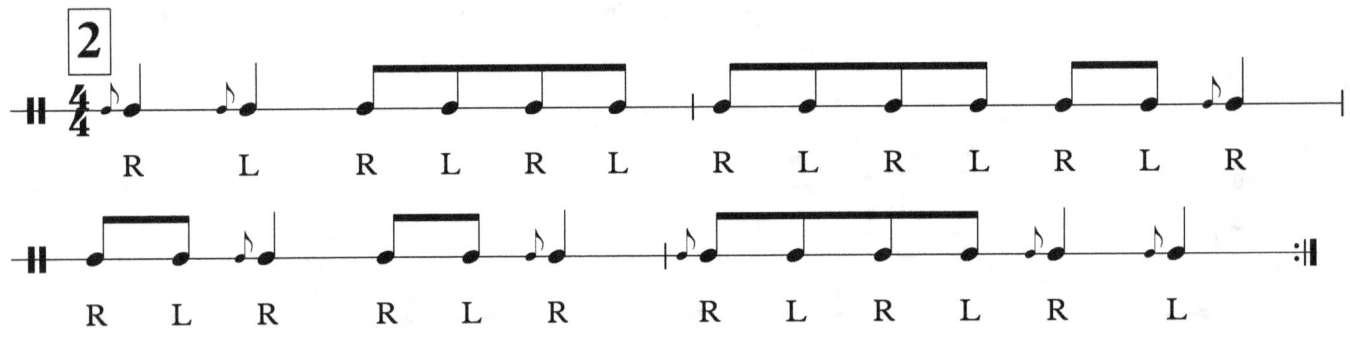

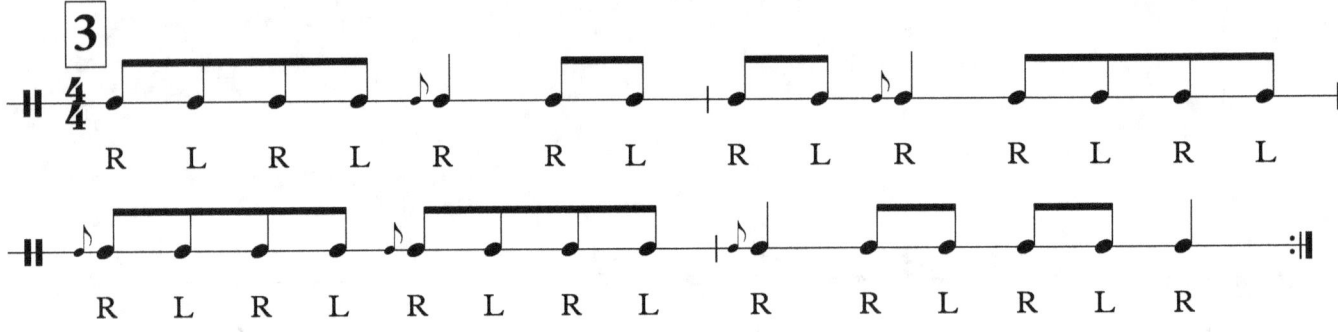

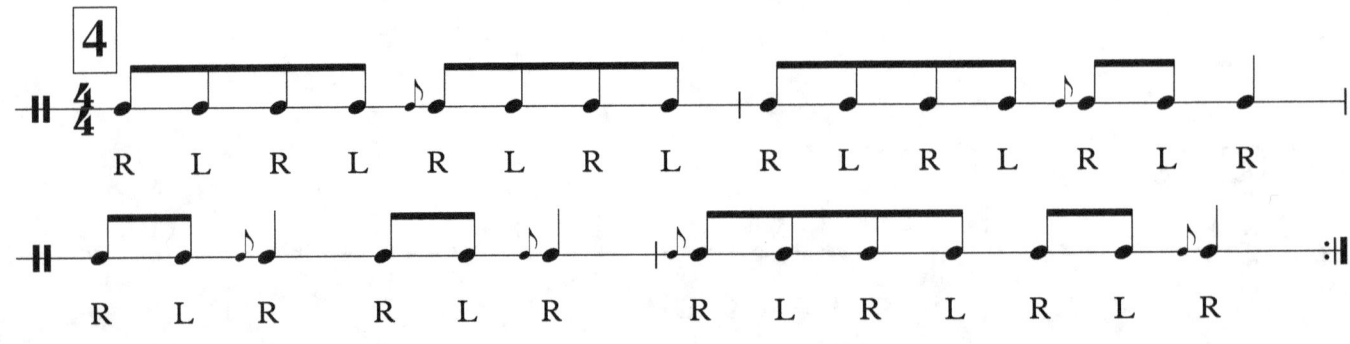

Lesson 12.4

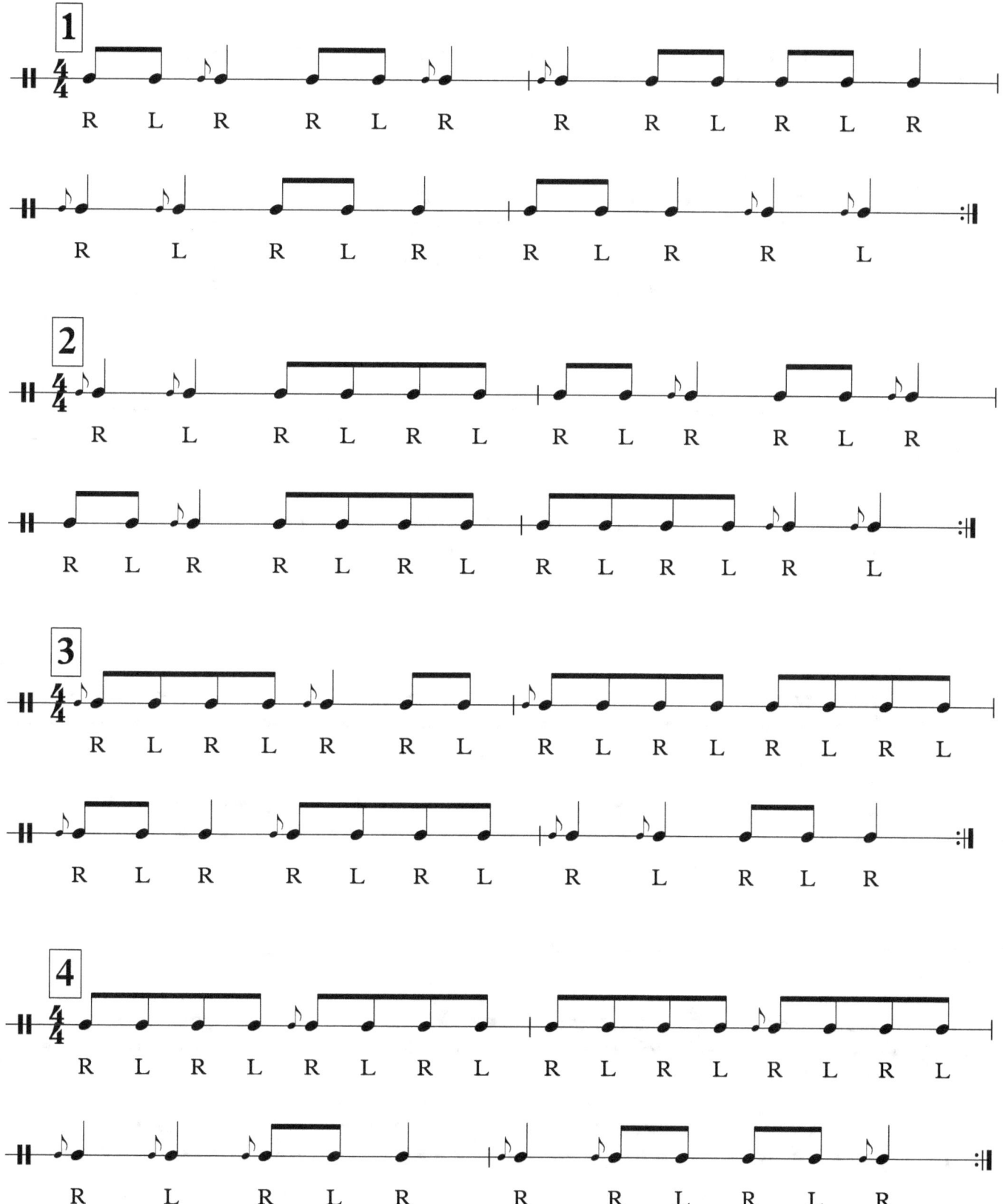

Lesson 12.5

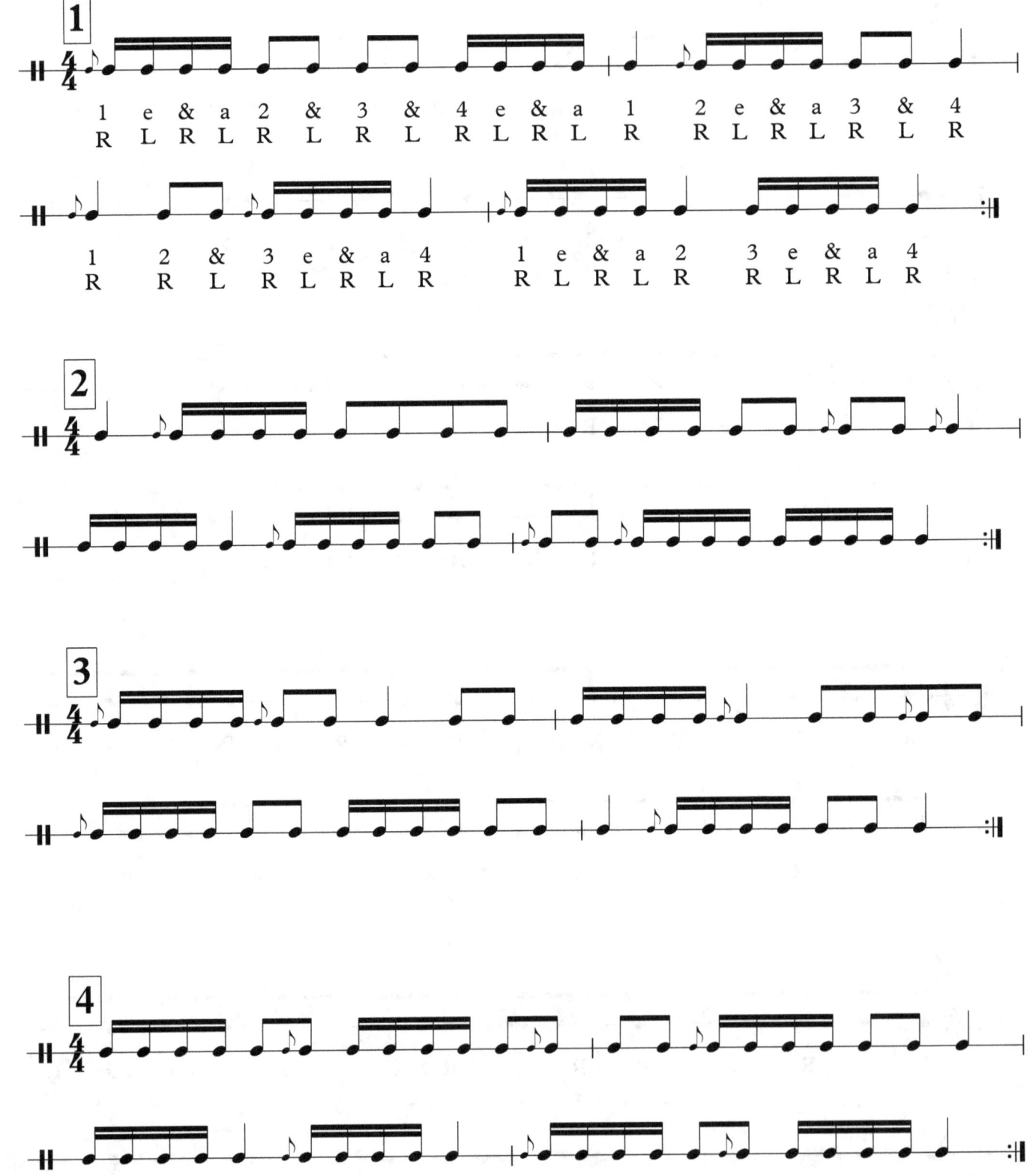

Foundational Snare Drumming
Finale!

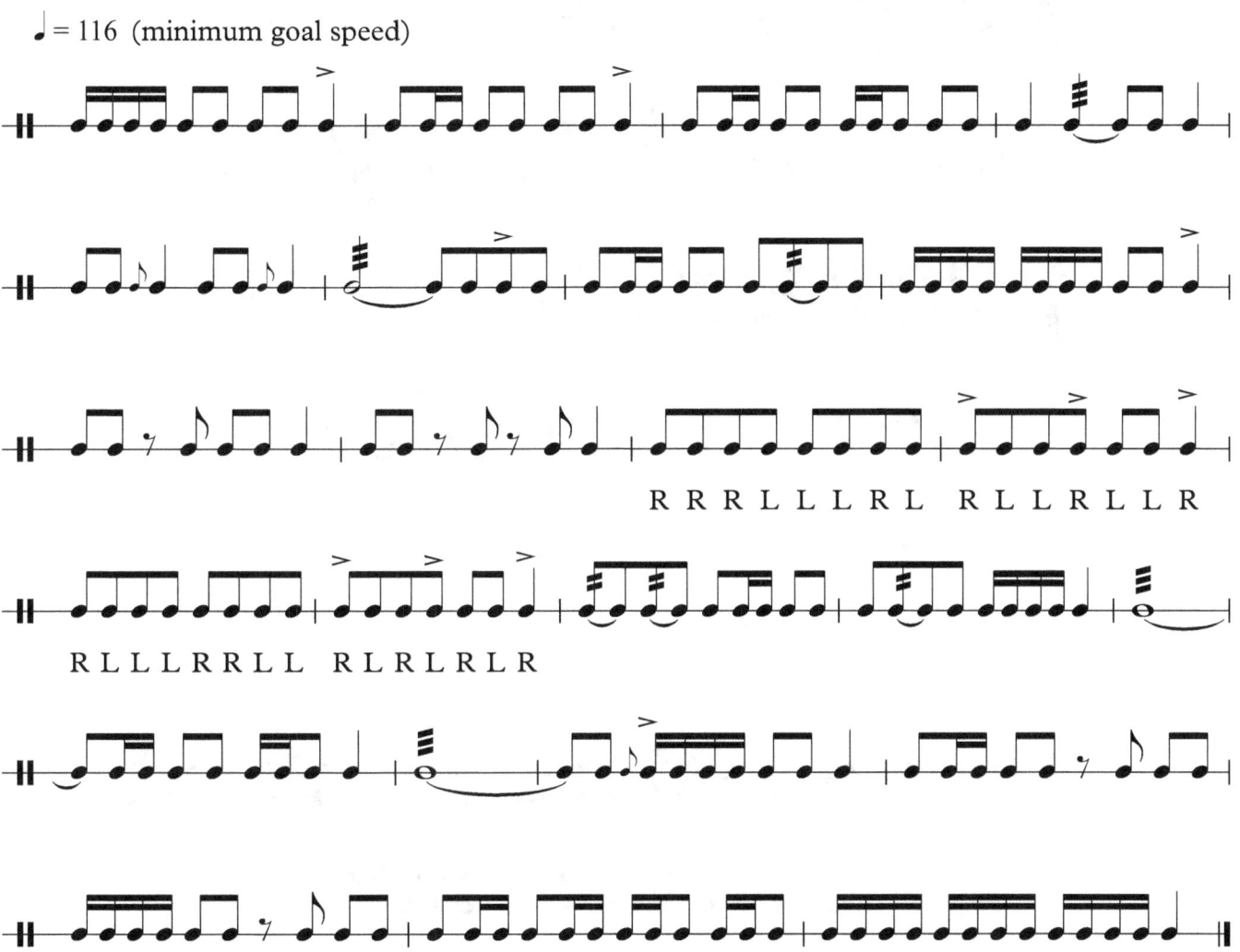

The following pages/exercises are to help you prepare for your next book –

"Foundations In Total Percussion"

The Double Stroke Roll:

The following is the "beginner" technique for double stroke rolls.

PINCH: You are still going to pinch the fulcrum, but not as tightly as you would to perform a multiple bounce roll.

Drop: You are going to drop your back three fingers just like when you played a multiple bounce roll.

Wrist: Instead of using your arm like you did with the multiple bounce roll, in a double stroke roll you are going to use your WRIST.

The goal is to let the stick bounce just twice with each wrist stroke. Here is an exercise to practice to help improve your double stroke rolls.

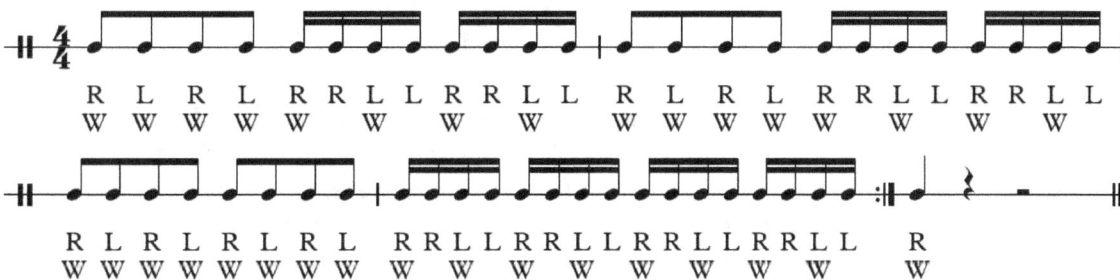

The "W's" are wrist strokes. Notice that the double strokes are exactly twice as fast as the wrist strokes. Double strokes are a rhythm, not just sustained sound. Another way to notate the above exercise is written below. The single slashes on the stem mean to double each note with the same hand exactly twice as fast as the notated rhythm. Both exercises should sound exactly the same.

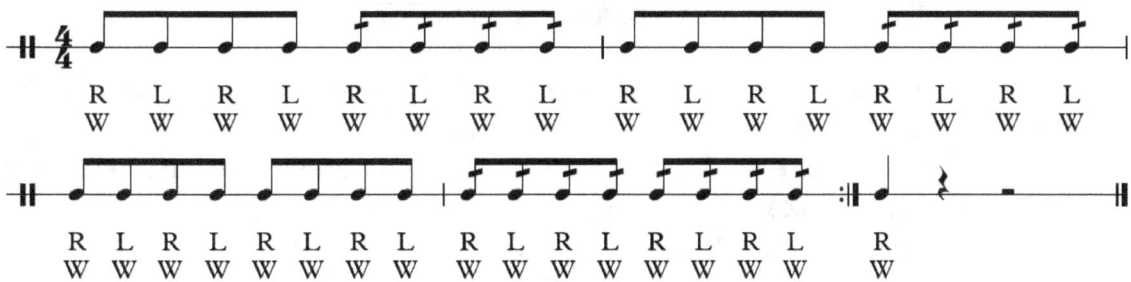

Your first two RUDIMENTS!

"Rudiments" are sticking patterns on the snare drum. There are two rudiments to focus on before moving on to the next book – The "Single Paradiddle" and the "Flam Tap".

The Single Paradiddle:

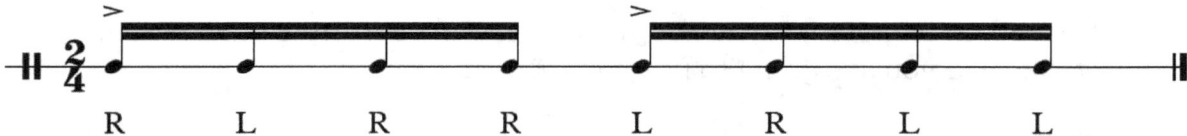

R   L   R   R   L   R   L   L

Couple things to think about when practicing the Single Paradiddle:

- First, check out the sticking pattern. This is actually an example of two Single Paradiddles. Single Paradiddles can start on the left hand or the right hand.
- Take note of the accent at the beginning of each Single Paradiddle.
  - It is important to play a downstroke on that accent and then relax that hand for the upcoming two consecutive strokes.
  - The second note of each paradiddle should be played as an upstroke.
  - Review the downstroke and upstroke before playing the paradiddle.

The Flam Tap:

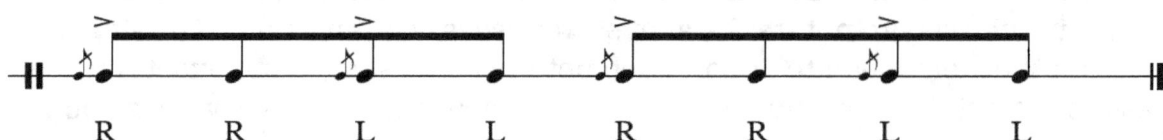

R   R   L   L   R   R   L   L

Couple things to think about when practicing the Flam Taps:

- Start by practicing each hand separately. Play 3 strokes in a row on each hand with each successive stroke getting lower.
  - The first stroke will be the accent. The second stroke with be the tap. The final stroke will be the grace not for the next flam.
- Keep your grace notes LOW!
- Start very slowly!

Preparing to read music on the Mallet Percussion

Musical Staff:

The Staff has 5 lines and 4 spaces

Musical Clefs:

First is the **Treble Clef.** This is the clef used for higher pitched instruments and is the clef you will use when learning mallet percussion.

A good saying to remember the Lines of the Treble Clef is:
Every **G**ood **B**urger **D**eserves **F**ries.

The spaces of the Treble Clef spell **F-A-C-E**.

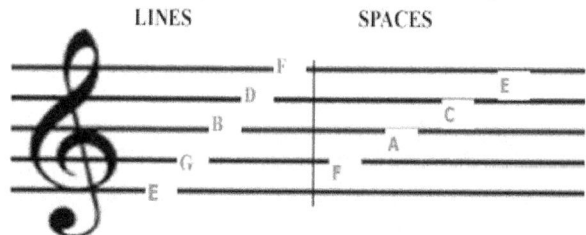

Next is the **Bass Clef.** This is the clef used for lower instruments and is the clef you will use for learning Timpani.

A good saying to remember the lines of the Bass Clef is:
Good **B**oys **D**o **F**ine **A**lways

A good saying to remember the spaces of the bass clef is:
All **C**ows **E**at **G**rass

Note Reading Practice
LABEL ALL OF THE NOTES!

Treble Clef Reading Practice:

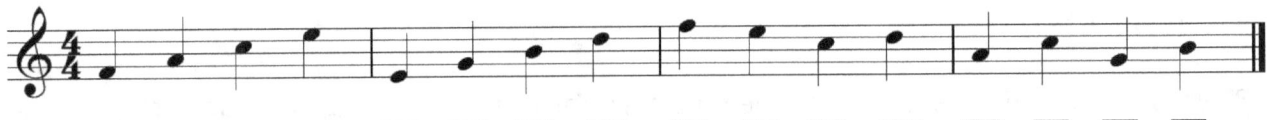

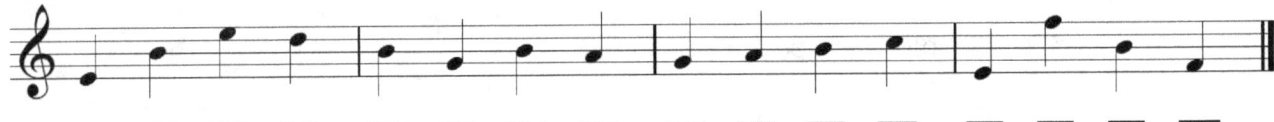

Bass Clef Reading Practice:

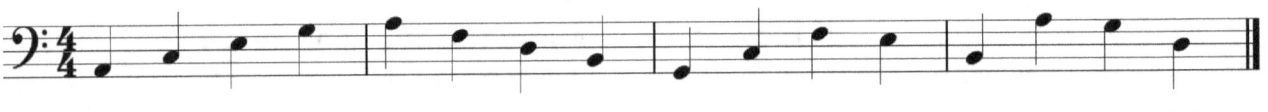

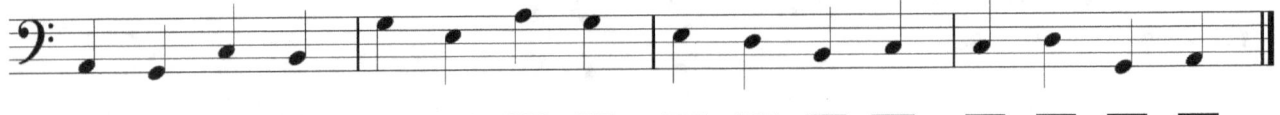

Learning the Keyboard

The raised keys are called ACCIDENTALS and are arranged by groups of two or three.

The lower keys are called NATURALS

A Flat Sign

♭

A Flat Sign lowers the pitch of a note one HALF STEP. A half step is the distance from one key to the next closest key to it (above or below). If a note is "flat" you will find it on the raised keys.

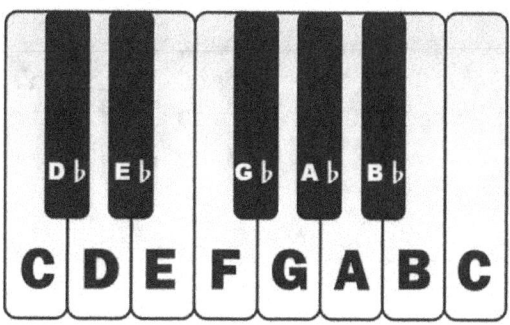

The Mallet Grip and Stroke

The mallet grip is very similar to the snare drum grip you already know.

- Have the mallet run diagonally across your palm like you did with the snare stick.
- Pinch the mallet between your pointer finger and thumb.
  - The pinch should happen right at the first knuckle of your pointer finger and the pad of your thumb.
- Wrap the remaining three fingers gently around the mallet. They should have a "feathers" touch with your palm.

The mallet stroke is similar to a snare stroke, but definitely has some different aspects to it.

- The mallet stroke consists of a downstroke AND an upstroke.
- Mallet percussion instruments have very little rebound unlike a snare drum.
  - This means you will need to put more energy into the upstroke then you are used to.
  - Both the downstroke and the upstroke should be relaxed and this should be a smooth motion.

For a video demonstration, go to the following link: https://safeyoutube.net/w/L8Hp

---

The Timpani Grip and Stroke

The Timpani Grip is similar to the mallet grip with one major difference.

- Grip the timpani mallet like you would a mallet but then rotate your hand so your thumb is facing the ceiling.
  - This is known as the French Grip.
- The back three fingers should gently rest on the shaft of the mallet.

The Timpani Stroke has many layers to it. We are going to start with just a basic stroke and will add to it as you advance.

- First and foremost, be as relaxed as possible.
  - Pretend to cast a fishing line towards the drum's head.
  - After impact let the mallet return to the starting height of the stroke.

For a video on the Timpani grip and Stroke, go to the following link: https://safeyoutube.net/w/f9Hp

www.ingramcontent.com/pod-product-compliance
Lightning Source LLC
Chambersburg PA
CBHW081157180526
45170CB00006B/2115